Best Friends' Stylish Spaces

Hi! Welcome to our world of fun and fantastic decorating ideas. We're the So Girly!™ teens and we've put together a whole houseful of room and space ideas … one specially decorated to fit each of our individual personalities. Turn the page to check out MacKenzie's Room, Avery's Closet, Kendra's Reading Nook, Chloë's Bath, Jessie's Room, Destiny's Corner, Jade's Phone Booth, and Brooke's Study. Let the So Girly!™ power add some razzle-dazzle to your space. And don't forget … your space is all about you, so feel free to mix, match, and change colors to fit your style.

How cool is that … and how positively GLAM!

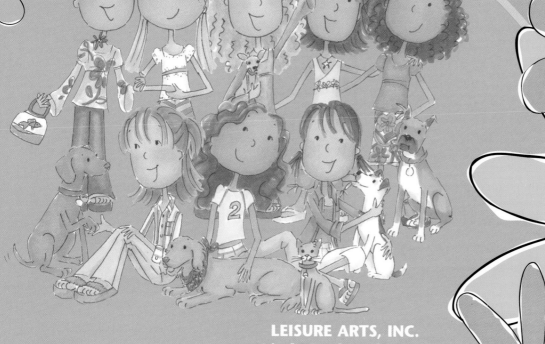

LEISURE ARTS, INC.
Little Rock, Arkansas

EDITORIAL STAFF

Vice President, Editor-in-Chief: Sandra Graham Case
Executive Director of Publications: Cheryl Nodine Gunnells
Senior Director of Publications: Susan White Sullivan
Director of Designer Relations: Debra Nettles
Senior Design Director: Cyndi Hansen
Editorial Director: Susan Frantz Wiles
Senior Director of Public Relations and Retail Marketing:
    Stephen Wilson
Senior Art Operations Director: Jeff Curtis
Design Director: Diana Sanders Cates
Craft Publications Director: Kristine Anderson Mertes
Art Publications Director: Rhonda Hodge Shelby
Art Imaging Director: Mark Hawkins

DESIGN

Designers: Cherece Athy, Tonya Bradford Bates,
    Polly Tullis Browning, Linda Butler, Kim Kern,
    Anne Pulliam Stocks, Linda Tiano, Lori Wenger,
    and Becky Werle

TECHNICAL

Technical Editor: Jennifer S. Hutchings
Technical Writers: Laura Siar Holyfield,
    Michelle Mullman James, and Christina Kirkendoll

EDITORIAL

Associate Editor: Steve Cooper

ART

Art Category Manager: Lora Puls
Graphic Artist: Andrea A. Amerson
Imaging Technicians: Steph Johnson and
    Mark Russell Potter
Staff Photographer: Lloyd Litsey
Photography Manager: Karen Hall
Photography Stylist: Janna B. Laughlin
Publishing Systems Administrator: Becky Riddle
Publishing Systems Assistants: Clint Hanson, John Rose,
    and Chris Wertenberger

BUSINESS STAFF

Publisher: Rick Barton
Vice President, Finance: Tom Siebenmorgen
Director of Corporate Planning and Development:
    Laticia Mull Dittrich
Vice President, Retail Marketing: Bob Humphrey
Vice President, Sales: Ray Shelgosh
Vice President, National Accounts: Pam Stebbins
Director of Sales and Services: Margaret Reinold
Vice President, Operations: Jim Dittrich
Comptroller, Operations: Rob Thieme
Retail Customer Service Manager: Stan Raynor
Print Production Manager: Fred F. Pruss

MacKenzie's Room

Jessie's Room

so girly

Table of Contents

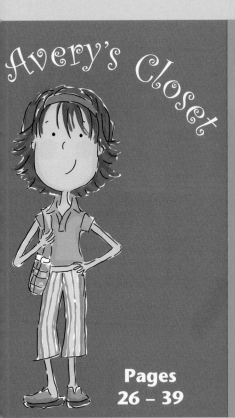
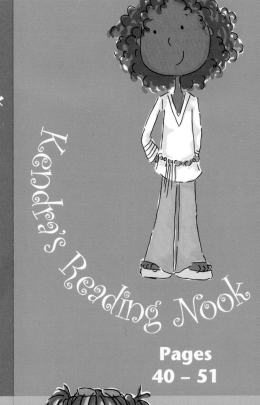

MacKenzie's Room

Hi, I'm MacKenzie, and welcome to my room. Let me tell you a little about myself. I'm on the Student Council, and I make sure I stay on top of all the groovy trends.

So, when I made over my bedroom, I really wanted something dazzling, you know — chic and with tons of girl power attitude. Check out my new headboard, done up in flashy So Girly!™ print fabrics with the matching vanity and cube seat … and that lamp that looks like a purse? Who'd have thought!

The painted canvases are so fun to mix, match, and rearrange. Oh! and my favorite: a cushy, comfy flower rug that keeps my toes tantalized. Cool, huh? Well, I'd better curl up under my princess throw and hit the books. Catch you later!

MacKenzie

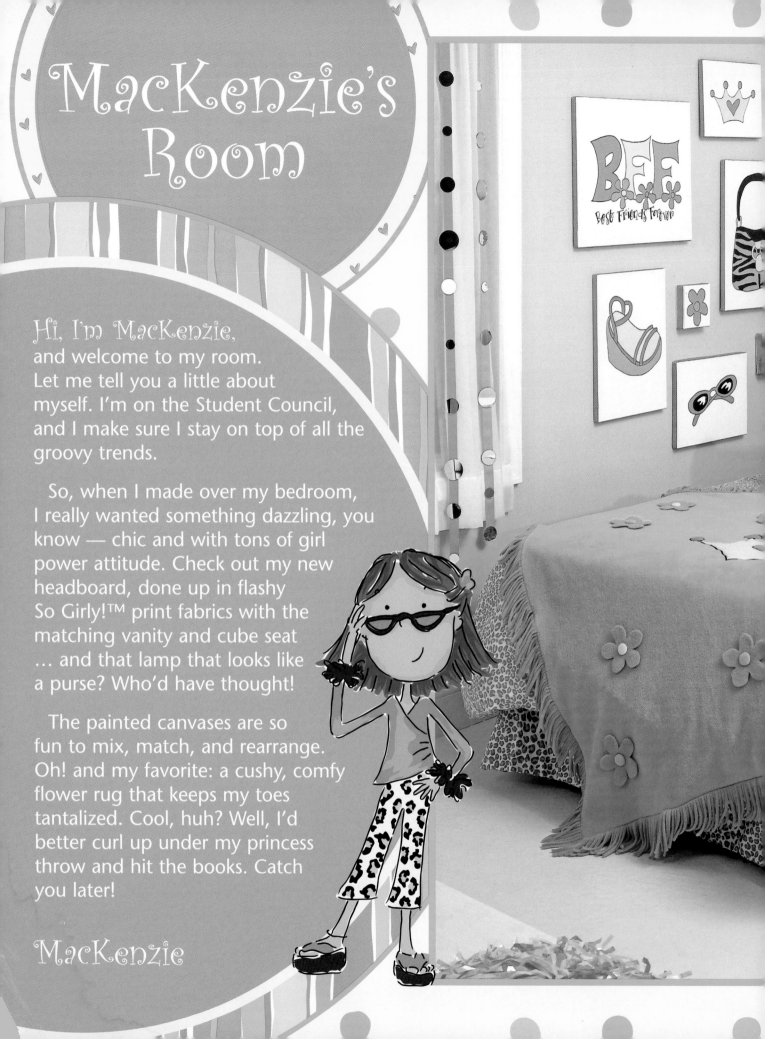

20" x 42" x 29" vanity table
1¼ yds pink print fabric
3½ yds me & my BiG ideas® print
   fabric for skirt
16" square of purple fabric
⅞ yd green striped fabric
16" square of pink dotted fabric
6¾ yds of 3/16" dia. cotton cord
3¼ yds pink ball fringe

Yardages are based on fabric with a 40" usable width. Match right sides and use a ¹/₂" seam allowance for all sewing.

1. Place top of vanity on wrong side of pink print fabric; draw around vanity top. Cut fabric ¹/₂" outside drawn line.

2. Follow **Continuous Bias Binding**, page 111, to make one 114" length of 2"w bias binding from purple fabric square and one 124" length of 2"w bias binding from pink dotted fabric square. Cut a 114" and a 123" length of cord.

3. To make purple welting, press one end of purple bias strip ¹/₂" to wrong side. Beginning ¹/₂" from pressed end, center 114" long cord on wrong side of strip. Matching long edges, fold strip over cord. Using zipper foot, sew next to cord. Trim flange to ¹/₂".

4. Beginning and ending 2" from welting ends and matching raw edges, pin flange of welting to right side of pink fabric piece. Trimming to fit, insert unfinished end of welting into folded end of welting. Finish pinning welting to fabric; baste. Pin and baste flange of ball fringe to fabric. Clip curves.

5. To make pink welting, center 123" length of cord on wrong side of pink bias strip. Matching long edges, fold strip over cord. Using zipper foot, sew next to cord. Trim flange to ¹/₂".

6. Cut a 25" x 124" piece from skirt fabric. Cut a 6¾" x 124" piece from green striped fabric (fabric will need to be pieced). Matching raw edges, baste flange of pink welting to one long edge of skirt fabric. Stitching close to welting, sew green striped piece to skirt fabric.

7. Press ends of skirt ¹/₄" to wrong side twice; topstitch. Press bottom edge ¹/₄" to wrong side. Press 1" to wrong side again and hem. Stopping and starting every 30" or so to keep threads from breaking, baste 3/8" and ¹/₄" from top raw edge of skirt. Pull basting threads to loosely gather skirt fabric. Beginning at center front and overlapping edges, pin, then sew gathered edge of skirt fabric to pink fabric. Turn cover right side out.

Sassy

1 yd green striped fabric
1/2 yd pink print fabric
1 5/8 yds pink ball fringe
1 5/8 yds purple marabou boa
14" cube ottoman

Yardages are based on fabric with a 40" usable width. Match right sides and use a 1/2" seam allowance for all sewing.

1. Cut four 15" squares from green striped fabric and one from pink print fabric. Beginning 1/2" from top edges, sew green fabric pieces together to form a tube; press seam allowance open.

2. Easing fabric to fit at corners, pin pink fabric square to top of tube; sew in place. Press bottom edge of cover 1/2" to wrong side; turn cover right side out. Pin flange of ball fringe to wrong side along bottom edge; trim excess fringe and topstitch in place.

3. Whipstitch marabou boa around top edges of cover.

4. Place cover on ottoman.

Hello!

$^7/_8$"w pink, purple, and yellow grosgrain ribbon
sheer curtains
hot glue gun
1", $1^1/_2$", and 2" dia. mirrors

1. Cut ribbon lengths the height of curtain plus 10".

2. Leaving 7" at one end of each ribbon undecorated, hot glue mirrors to each ribbon length as desired. Folding $3^1/_2$" of undecorated end of each ribbon length to the wrong side, arrange and pin ribbons on curtain. Catching ribbon ends in stitching, topstitch across ribbons along bottom of rod pocket.

3. Fold and hot glue bottom ends of ribbons $^1/_4$" to wrong side.

Flower Pillow

³/₄ yd pink print fabric
scrap of yellow print fabric
paper-backed fusible web
yellow thread for appliqué
polyester fiberfill

Yardage is based on fabric with a 40"
usable width. Match right sides and use a
¹/₂" seam allowance for all sewing.

1. Using a photocopier, enlarge flower pattern, page 22, as indicated on pattern. Use pattern to cut two flowers (one in reverse) from pink fabric. Cut a 3" x 68" strip from pink fabric (fabric will need to be pieced). Draw over flower center on paper side of fusible web. Fuse web pattern to wrong side of yellow print fabric; cut out appliqué along drawn line and remove paper backing. Arrange and fuse appliqué on pillow top.

2. Refer to Steps 2–3 of Heart Pillow, page 11, to sew flower center appliqué to pillow top and to assemble pillow.

Neck Roll Pillow

1/2 yd yellow print fabric
compass
transfer paper
black medium-point permanent pen
6" dia. x 15" neck roll
1 1/8 yds purple marabou boa

Yardage is based on fabric with a 40" usable width. Match right sides and use a 1/2" seam allowance for all sewing.

1. Use compass to mark two 7" dia. circles on fabric; cut out. Cut a 16" x 20" piece from fabric.
2. Using a photocopier, enlarge pattern, page 24, as indicated on pattern. Transfer pattern onto fabric rectangle (**Fig. 1**). Draw over words with permanent pen.

Fig. 1

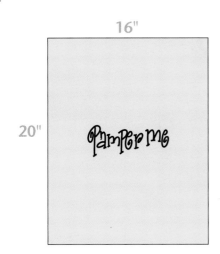

3. Leaving an opening in the center for inserting neck roll, sew short ends of rectangle together, forming a tube. Easing to fit, pin fabric circles to ends of tube. Sew circles to tube; clip curves. Turn pillow cover right side out. Insert neck roll; sew opening closed. Cut boa in half; whipstitch one length around each end of pillow.

Heart Pillow

5/8 yd green print fabric
1/8 yd dark green fabric
paper-backed fusible web
dark green thread for
   appliqués
polyester fiberfill

Yardages are based on fabric with a 40" usable width. Match right sides and use a 1/2" seam allowance for all sewing.

1. Using a photocopier, enlarge heart pattern, page 25, as indicated on pattern. Use pattern to cut two hearts (one in reverse) from green print fabric. Cut a 3" x 65" strip from green print fabric (fabric will need to be pieced). Turn pattern over and draw over spots on paper side of fusible web. Fuse web patterns to wrong side of dark green fabric; cut out appliqués along drawn lines and remove paper backing. Arrange and fuse appliqués on pillow top.
2. Follow **Machine Appliqué**, page 110, to sew appliqués onto pillow top.
3. Press one short end of fabric strip 1/2" to wrong side. Beginning with pressed end, pin strip to edge of pillow top. Overlapping ends by 2", trim excess fabric strip; sew in place. Leaving an opening for turning, sew pillow bottom to strip; turn right side out. Stuff with fiberfill; sew opening closed.

stretched canvases (we used three
    5" squares for flowers, 9" x 12" for
    crown, 10" x 14" for sunglasses,
    12" x 16" for sandal, 14" x 18" for
    purse, and 16" x 20" for "B.F.F.")
foam plate for palette
paintbrushes
white, fuchsia, dark yellow, green,
    blue, purple, and black acrylic paints
transfer paper
black medium-point permanent pen
matte clear acrylic sealer
    1"w purple dotted grosgrain ribbon
    fabric glue

Allow paint to dry after each application.
1. Paint each canvas white.
2. Using a photocopier, copy the
    desired patterns from pages 20-24
    as indicated on patterns. Transfer
    copied patterns onto canvases.
    Outline each pattern with pen.
3. Referring to photo, paint each
    canvas. Use pen to outline entire
    pattern again. Apply sealer to
    canvas; allow to dry.
4. Overlapping ends at center
    bottom, and aligning edge of
    ribbon with front of canvas, glue
    ribbon around sides of canvas.
    Wrap and glue any excess ribbon
    to the back.

1½ yds of 60"w green fleece
⅝ yd of 60"w pink fleece
⅛ yd of 60"w purple fleece
¼ yd of 60"w yellow fleece
scraps of blue fleece
tracing paper
freezer paper
wash-away double-sided sewing tape
black and green thread
eleven 1" dia. self-cover buttons
rotary cutter
cutting mat

1. For throw, cut a 50" square from green fleece; cut a ½" square from each corner of throw.

2. Using a photocopier, copy flower and crown patterns, pages 22 and 24, as indicated on patterns. Turn copied patterns over. Tracing flower 11 times, trace all patterns onto dull side of freezer paper; cut apart. Iron shiny side of freezer paper patterns to wrong side of fleece with a warm iron. Cut out freezer paper patterns; remove freezer paper.

3. Arrange crown pieces on center of throw. Use sewing tape to temporarily hold pieces in place.

Follow **Machine Appliqué**, page 110, to sew crown appliqués on throw.

4. Cover buttons with green and yellow fleece. Arrange flowers randomly on throw. To attach flowers to throw, sew a covered button through center of each flower.

5. For fringe, cutting selvage to selvage, cut four 4" x 49" strips from pink fleece. Matching right sides and long edges, zigzag stitch pink strips to edges of throw.

6. Cutting to within ⅛" of seam between fringe and throw, cut fringe into ¼"w strips.

rotary cutter
cutting mat
$3^1/_2$ yds of 60"w purple fleece
1 yd of 60"w pink fleece
$^1/_8$ yd of 60"w yellow fleece
tape
T-pin
yardstick
black medium-point permanent pen
40" square of Graph 'N Latch® rug
  canvas
40" square of cardboard
latch hook
non-skid backing (optional)

1. Use rotary cutter and mat to cut each fleece color into $^3/_4$"w lengthwise strips. (If cut selvage to selvage, fleece will stretch.) Cut each strip into 4" lengths.
2. Tape T-pin to yardstick at the 1" mark with point extending past bottom edge of yardstick. Tape pen to yardstick at the 18" mark with point extending past bottom edge of yardstick. Fold canvas in half, then fold in half again. Unfold canvas. Place canvas on cardboard. With T-pin at point where folds intersect, rotate yardstick to draw a 34" dia. circle on canvas with pen. To make a 2" border around outside edge of circle, move pen to the 16" mark on yardstick. Draw a 30" dia. circle inside first circle. Cut circle from canvas along outside line.
3. Using a photocopier, enlarge pattern, page 22, as indicated on pattern. Arrange pattern between canvas and cardboard so that pattern is centered on canvas; tape in place on cardboard. Use pen to outline pattern on canvas. Remove canvas from cardboard.
4. Clipping canvas as necessary, fold 2" outside border to the back. You will hook through both layers of canvas for a finished edge. To hook fleece onto canvas, begin on the top or bottom of canvas and slide hook beneath one cross bar in canvas. Wrap one fleece strip around hook with ends even (**Fig. 1**); slide hook back through canvas until strip is about halfway through.

Fig. 1

5. Leaving shaft of hook in loop, catch ends of strip in hook and pull them through the loop (**Fig. 2**). Pull knot tight (**Fig. 3**).

Fig. 2

Fig. 3

6. Work across the row, changing strip colors as necessary, before moving to the next row. Follow hooking pattern (**Fig. 4**) when filling the canvas to ensure having enough yardage to complete the rug.

Fig. 4

7. Apply non-skid backing material to back of rug if desired.

¹/₄ yd green and white polka-dot fabric
two 12" x 18" sheets of extra thick
  template plastic
spray adhesive
two 4" and two 7" dia. brass craft rings
pinking shears
craft knife
cutting mat
hot glue gun
20-gauge gold jewelry wire
wire cutters
fabric glue
³/₄ yd floral trim
³/₄" dia. pink button
¹/₄ yd of ¹/₈"w fuchsia grosgrain ribbon
18-gauge galvanized wire
needle-nose pliers
6mm pink faceted beads
17" length of pink marabou boa
120v clip light

*Yardage is based on fabric with a 40"
usable width. Use spray adhesive in a
well-ventilated area.*

1. For lamp sides, cut two 4³/₈" x 10¹/₂"
    strips each from fabric and template
    plastic. Use spray adhesive to glue
    fabric to plastic strips. Using a 4"
    ring as a guide, draw a half circle
    on one end of each strip (**Fig. 1**);
    cut out.

Fig. 1

2. For lamp front and back, draw
    around outside of a 7" ring twice
    each on fabric and template plastic;
    cut plastic along drawn lines and
    use pinking shears to cut fabric ¹/₄"
    outside drawn lines. Using spray
    adhesive and leaving fabric edges
    unglued, center and cover plastic
    circles with fabric. Use craft knife to
    cut a 1" dia. circle in center of one
    fabric-covered circle for lamp back;
    set aside.

3. Leaving a ¹/₂" space between curved
    ends of side strips at top and a 1¹/₂"
    space between straight ends at
    bottom of lamp, hot glue edges of
    strips between 7" rings (**Fig. 2**).

Fig. 2

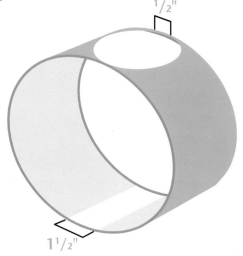

4. Wrapping several times, use gold
    wire to attach 4" rings to 7" rings
    around top and bottom openings.
    Hot glue plastic edges of lamp front
    and back to 7" rings; use fabric glue
    to adhere fabric edges to sides of
    lamp. Gluing outer edges of floral
    trim to lamp sides, use fabric glue
    to adhere trim along front edges of
    lamp.

5. Thread ribbon through button to the back. Hot glue button 2$^{1}/_{2}$" from top edge of lamp front; glue ribbon ends inside top of lamp.
6. For handle, cut a 20" length of galvanized wire. Use pliers to wrap each end around top 4" dia. ring. Cut a 3 yd length of gold wire.

Thread beads on gold wire, then secure one end at base of handle. Coil beaded wire around galvanized wire; secure remaining end.
7. Hot glue boa around top 4" dia. ring; glue ends together.
8. Insert clip light in back opening.

4' x 4½' piece of ½" thick
    plywood
drill with ³/₁₆" dia. bit
quilt batting
3 yds me & my BiG ideas® print
    fabric with character border
1¾ yds purple fabric
½"w tack stripping
staple gun
ten 1⅛" dia. self-cover buttons
ten ½" dia. buttons
upholstery needle
heavy-duty button and upholstery
    thread
4½ yds pink marabou boa

Yardages are based on fabric with a 40" usable width. We cut the character border from the bottom of our print fabric and sewed it along the top of the piece.

1. Referring to **Fig. 1** for hole placement, drill holes through plywood board.

Fig. 1

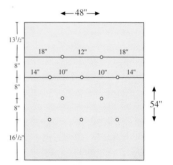

Angel

Pamper me

2. Cut a 56" x 62" piece each from batting and print fabric (this will need to be pieced).

3. Center and layer batting, then board on wrong side of pieced fabric. Wrapping batting and fabric to back of board, staple the center of each edge of fabric and batting to back of board. Working on opposite sides of the board, pulling fabric taut, and folding the fabric and batting to ease as needed, staple in place. Turn headboard right side up.

4. Draw lines 4" from all edges of headboard as indicated by pink dashed lines (**Fig. 2**). For side borders, cut two 8" x 60" strips each from purple fabric and batting. Matching right sides and centering fabric strip over headboard, align one long edge of each fabric strip along marked side lines.

Fig. 2

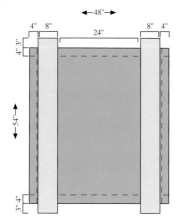

5. Place tack stripping along outer edges of each fabric strip; staple stripping in place. Place a batting strip on each fabric strip, then wrap batting and fabric to back of headboard. Pulling fabric taut, staple in place.

6. For top and bottom borders, cut two 8" x 52" strips from purple fabric and two 8" x 39" strips from batting. Press ends of fabric strips 1" to wrong side. Center and align fabric strips along remaining marked lines. Beginning and ending 4$\frac{1}{2}$" from side edges of headboard, place tack stripping along outer edges of each fabric strip; staple stripping in place. Center a batting strip on each fabric strip, then folding ends of fabric diagonally to wrong side to form mitered corners, wrap batting and fabric to back of headboard. Pulling fabric taut, staple in place.

7. Cover 1$\frac{1}{8}$" buttons with purple fabric. For each button, thread upholstery needle with two lengths of thread. Working from back of headboard, thread needle through $\frac{1}{2}$" dia. button, hole in headboard, and shank of covered button. Thread needle back through headboard and button; pull tight to tuft headboard and knot to secure.

8. Whipstitch boa along sides and top of headboard.

Perfect

Best Friends Forever

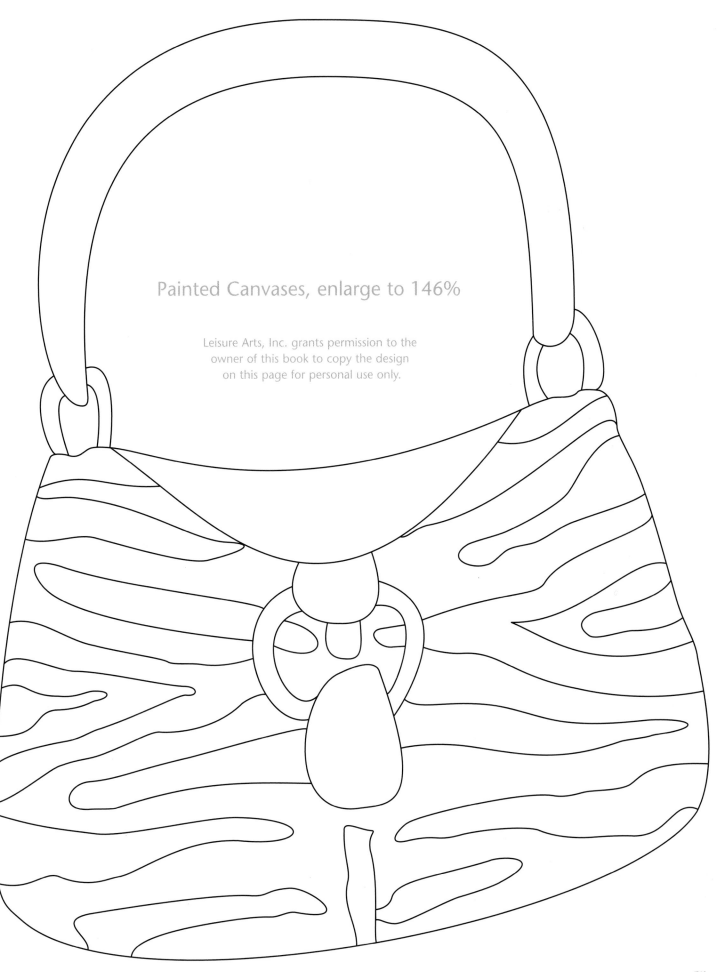

Painted Canvases, enlarge to 146%

Fleece Throw, reduce to 51%
Flower Pillow, enlarge to 206%
Hooked Fleece Rug, enlarge to 194%
Painted Canvases, reduce to 51%

22

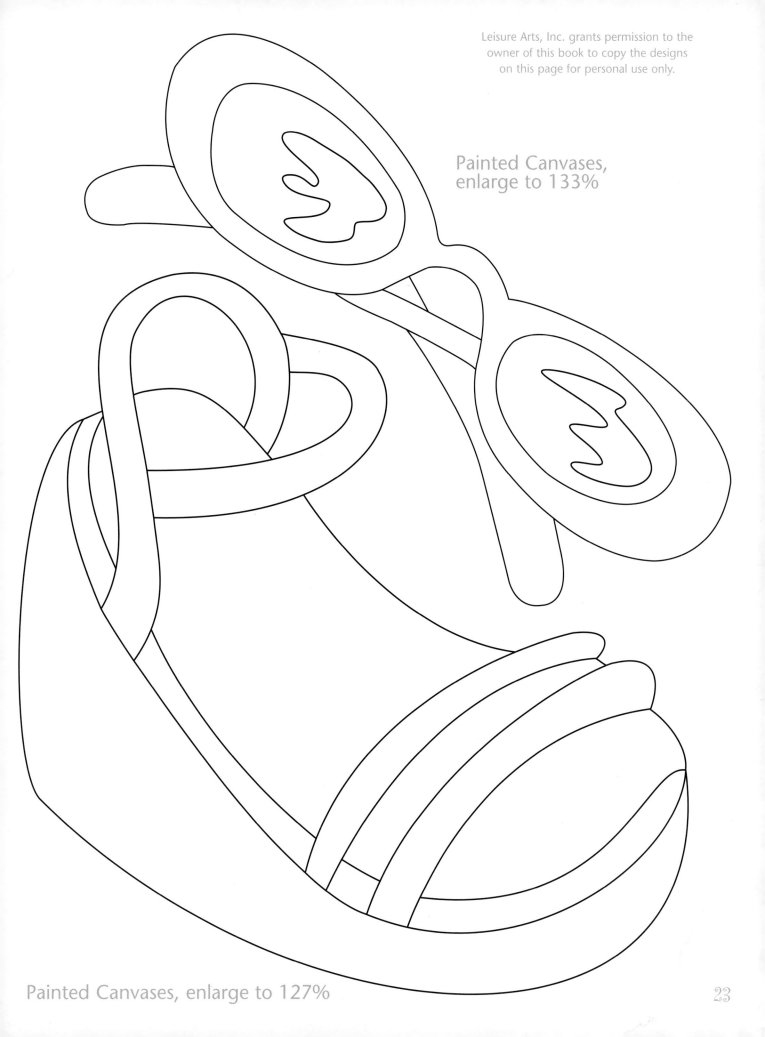

Painted Canvases,
enlarge to 133%

Painted Canvases, enlarge to 127%

Fleece Throw,
enlarge to 163%

Painted Canvases,
reduce to 90%

Neck Roll Pillow, enlarge to 126%

Pamper me

Heart Pillow, enlarge to 205%

Avery's Closet

I'm Avery, and I just returned from a long weekend of golfing in the Hamptons. While I'm unpacking, let me show you a few of the cool things in my closet.

The full-length mirror reflects my attitude all the way. The really big corkboard frame is perfect for pinning up magazine clippings, notes, photos, and stuff so I can stay updated on fashion and trends. My hanging caddy with painted flaps and the stacked boxes are great for organizing extra stuff … and that's just the beginning.

Go ahead, put some So Girly!™ razzle-dazzle into your closet. See … goes to show you that storing doesn't have to be boring!

Avery

fabric glue
spray adhesive
Square Box:
  $4^1/_2$"w x $4^1/_2$"d x $2^1/_2$"h box with lid
  $^1/_8$ yd orange fabric
  9" square of pink print fabric
  tracing paper
  craft knife
  cutting mat
  $^3/_4$ yd of 2"w sheer orange check
    ribbon
  So Girly!™ IdeaStix™
Hexagonal Box:
  8"w x 9"d x 4"h hexagonal box
    with lid
  $^1/_4$ yd yellow fabric
  $^1/_3$ yd yellow print fabric
  1 yd pink ball fringe
  1 yd sheer yellow check ribbon
  So Girly!™ IdeaStix™
Round Box:
  10" dia. x 5"h box with lid
  $^1/_4$ yd pink print fabric
  $^3/_8$ yd floral fabric
  3" x 9" piece of yellow dotted fabric
  fusible interfacing
  tracing paper
  transfer paper
  green, blue, and white acrylic paints
  paintbrushes
  black fine-point permanent pen
  orange mini rickrack
  pink embroidery floss
  four $^5/_8$" dia. orange buttons

Yardages are based on fabric with a 40" usable width. Use spray adhesive in a well-ventilated area.

1. To cover each box with fabric, measure height of box, then measure around box and add 1" to each measurement; cut a fabric strip the determined size. Fold and glue one end of strip $^1/_2$" to wrong side.

2. Leaving $^1/_2$" of fabric at top and bottom and overlapping ends at back, use spray adhesive to apply fabric to box. Folding and clipping as needed, glue fabric edges to bottom and inside of box.

3. For square box lid, use pattern, page 39, and craft knife to cut scallops along edges of lid.

4. Draw around top of lid on wrong side of fabric and add $^1/_2$" to all sides; cut out. Wrapping excess to sides and clipping as needed, use spray adhesive to apply fabric to top of lid. Measure around lid; add 1". Measure height of lid; add $^1/_2$". Cut a fabric strip the determined size. Fold and glue one end $^1/_2$" to wrong side. With one long edge of strip even with top of lid and overlapping ends at back, adhere strip around lid. Clipping fabric as needed, glue excess fabric to inside of lid.

5. Cut ribbon length in half; glue one end of each length under opposite sides of lid. Tie ribbon into a bow and trim ends. Apply IdeaStix to sides of box.

6. For hexagonal box lid, follow Step 4 to apply fabric to lid. Glue ball fringe, then ribbon along edges of lid. Apply IdeaStix to sides of box.

7. For round box lid, follow Step 4 to apply fabric to lid. Fuse interfacing to dotted fabric; trim to $2^1/_2$" x 8". Using a photocopier, enlarge pattern, page 38, as indicated on pattern. Transfer pattern onto fabric. Refer to photo to paint design; allow to dry. Outline and add details with pen. Glue painted design, then rickrack border to box. Thread floss through each button; knot on back and glue to box.

hanging canvas organizer
canvas fabric
3/8"w fusible web tape
transfer paper
white, pink, yellow, and orange
  acrylic paints
paintbrushes
black fine-point permanent pen
three pom-pom trims
craft glue
six 3/4" dia. buttons of assorted colors

Allow paint to dry after each application. Use a 1/4" seam allowance for all sewing unless otherwise noted.

1. Measure height and width of one opening of organizer. Add 1" to each measurement and cut three pieces of canvas fabric this size.

2. Fuse web tape along two opposite edges on wrong side of each fabric piece. Remove paper backing and press edges 1/2" to wrong side. Repeat for remaining edges.

3. Using a photocopier, enlarge patterns, pages 38 and 39, as indicated on patterns. Transfer one pattern to each fabric piece. Refer to photo to paint designs; outline with pen.

4. Cut two lengths of pom-pom trim to fit across each fabric piece. Alternating pom-poms, layer and glue two trims along bottom back of each fabric piece.

5. Cut six 3 1/2" x 4" tabs from canvas fabric. Fold each tab in half lengthwise; sew along long raw edges. Press tab so that seam is at center back; sew along one end. Clip corners and turn tab right side out. Press raw ends 1/4" to inside; topstitch end closed.

6. Glue two tabs to the top of each fabric piece; glue a button to the bottom of each tab. Glue the tab tops to the organizer so fabric pieces drape over front of organizer.

canvas clothes hamper
white primer
yellow, orange, red, and fuchsia
  acrylic paints
paintbrush
matte clear acrylic sealer
black fine-point permanent pen
stencil plastic
craft knife
cutting mat
thick corrugated cardboard
stencil adhesive
stencil brush

Allow paint and sealer to dry after each application. Use stencil adhesive in a well-ventilated area.

1. Remove fabric from hamper stand. Prime, then paint stand yellow. Apply sealer.
2. Using a photocopier, enlarge pattern, page 38, as indicated on pattern. Use pen to trace three flowers (one for each color) and one flower center onto stencil plastic. Use craft knife to cut stencils from plastic.
3. Working on one side of hamper fabric at a time, place cardboard on wrong side of area to be stenciled. Apply stencil adhesive to back of flower stencil; adhere stencil to fabric.
4. Dip stencil brush in paint, then lightly pat brush on a paper towel to remove excess paint. To prevent paint from bleeding under edge of stencil, use an up and down motion and pounce a light coat of paint over flower stencil. Repeat to apply a second light coat of paint; remove stencil. Stencil remaining flowers, then flower centers. Outline flowers and centers with pen.
5. Dip handle end of stencil brush in paint to add dots to hamper fabric.

Girl Power

1 1/8 yds yellow dotted fabric
fusible interfacing
flat wooden clothes hanger
1/3 yd floral fabric
1/3 yd fuchsia fabric
1 5/8 yds of 1/4" dia. cotton cord
1/4 yd orange fabric
paper-backed fusible web
orange thread

Yardages are based on fabric with a 40" usable width. Match right sides and use a ¹/₂" seam allowance for all sewing.

1. For front and back, cut two 19" x 36" pieces from dotted fabric and fusible interfacing. Iron interfacing to wrong side of fabric pieces. Place fabric pieces right sides together. Refer to **Fig. 1** to place hanger on fabric pieces and mark angle lines with a pencil. Remove hanger; trim fabric to ¹/₂" above drawn lines.

Fig. 1

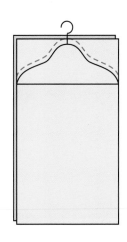

2. Cut two 8³/₄" x 19" pocket pieces from floral fabric and one from fuchsia fabric. For welting, cut three 18" lengths of cord and three 2¹/₂" x 19" strips from orange fabric.

3. To make each length of welting, center one cord length on wrong side of one fabric strip. Matching long edges, fold strip over cord. Using a zipper foot, sew next to cord. Trim flange to ¹/₂".

4. Matching raw edges, sew a length of welting along one long edge on front of each pocket piece. Press flange to wrong side of pocket piece.

5. Using a photocopier, enlarge pattern, page 38, as indicated on pattern. Trace three flowers and flower centers onto paper side of fusible web. Fuse web patterns to wrong side of orange and dotted fabrics; cut out appliqués along drawn lines and remove paper backing. Arrange and fuse two appliqués on fuchsia pocket piece and remaining appliqué 1" from top of front piece. Using orange thread, follow **Machine Appliqué**, page 110, to sew around flowers and flower centers.

6. Matching right sides, pin bottom edge of fuchsia pocket piece 11³/₄" from bottom of front piece (**Fig. 2**). Sew along pinned edge; press pocket to right side and baste ends of pocket to front piece. Measuring 11¹/₄" from bottom of fuchsia pocket, repeat for top floral pocket. Place remaining floral pocket, right side up, at bottom of front piece; baste along bottom and ends of pocket.

Fig. 2

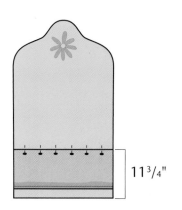

11³/₄"

7. For pocket dividers, topstitch 6¹/₂" from each end of top pocket and along center of remaining pockets.

8. Leaving a 1" opening at center top and a 10" opening at the bottom, sew back piece to front piece. Clip corners and curves and turn right side out; press. Insert hanger and sew bottom opening closed.

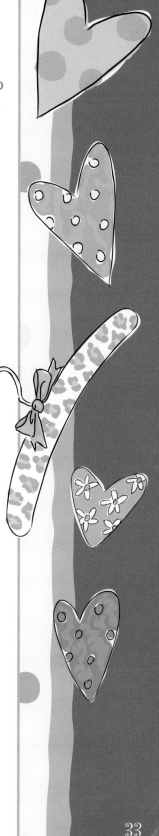

33

Heartbreaker

cute purses!

Audra
952-5853

green!

Spring Fling = find a dress!

six 8" x 36½" self-adhesive cork panels
  with rounded edges
box knife
transfer paper
red, fuchsia, yellow, orange, and white
  acrylic paints
paintbrushes
black broad-point permanent pen
1¾ yds of ⅝"w pink grosgrain ribbon
framed wall mirror with hanging
  hardware
removable tape
craft glue
So Girly!™ IdeaStix™

Allow paint to dry after each application.

1. For top and bottom borders,
   measure width of mirror; add 16".
   Cut two cork panels the determined
   measurement. For each side border,
   measure height of mirror; add 16".
   Butt two cork panels together and
   trim to determined measurement.

2. For mitered corners on top and
   bottom borders, measure and mark
   8" from ends on one long side of
   each border. Draw a line from each
   mark to opposite corner; cut along
   this line (**Fig. 1**).

Fig. 1

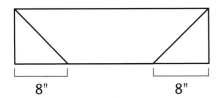

   8"   8"

3. For mitered corners on each side
   border, keep ends butted together
   and follow Step 2 to measure and
   cut outer ends of each side border.

4. Use a photocopier to enlarge pattern,
   page 38, as indicated on pattern.
   Transfer pattern onto center of top
   border. Refer to photo to paint
   design. Outline with pen.

5. On remaining borders, paint stripes
   of varying widths and colors. Outline
   each stripe with pen.

6. Cut four 14" lengths of ribbon; glue
   one end of each length to a corner
   on back of mirror and tape
   remaining end to front of mirror.
   Leaving room for bottom cork
   border, hang mirror on wall.

7. With "Heartbreaker" design at top,
   use self-adhesive strips on cork
   borders to adhere borders to wall
   around mirror (**Fig. 2**).

Fig. 2

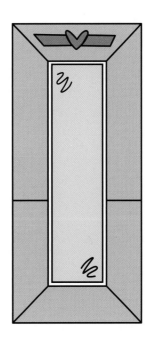

8. Remove tape and glue ribbons along
   mitered corners of cork; wrap and
   glue to back.

9. Adhere IdeaStix to mirror.

wooden tilt shoe rack cabinet
sandpaper
light yellow spray paint for plastic
transfer paper
pink, black, white, yellow, and fuchsia
  acrylic paints
paintbrushes
So Girly!™ pre-pasted wallpaper
  border
assorted sizes of round foam brushes
matte clear acrylic sealer

Use spray paint in a well-ventilated area. Allow paint and sealer to dry after each application.

1. Lightly sand, then spray paint cabinet yellow.
2. Using a photocopier, enlarge pattern, page 39, as indicated on pattern. Transfer pattern to front of cabinet. Refer to photo to paint flower and background.
3. Cut strips of wallpaper border to overlap flower by 2" and reach to sides of cabinet. Cut out flower background pattern from Step 2; use pattern to cut curves on wallpaper border to match curves of flower background. Follow manufacturer's instructions to adhere border to front of cabinet.
4. Cut border strips to fit along sides and back of cabinet; adhere to cabinet.
5. Paint a black stripe above and below edges of wallpaper border strips. Use foam brushes to paint polka-dots on bottom front and top of cabinet.
6. Apply sealer to cabinet.

three-drawer organizer
light yellow spray paint for plastic
transfer paper
black, white, yellow, and pink acrylic
  paints
paintbrushes
So Girly!™ wallpaper border
double-stick tape
So Girly!™ scrapbook papers for
  drawer fronts
three 4^1/$_2$" x 3^1/$_4$" tags
scrapbook papers for tags
pink cardstock
So Girly!™ IdeaStix™

Use spray paint in a well-ventilated area. Allow paint to dry after each application.

1. Remove drawers; spray paint organizer.
2. Using a photocopier, enlarge pattern, page 39, as indicated on pattern. Transfer pattern onto top of organizer; paint flower.
3. Cut out icons from wallpaper border; use tape to adhere icons to sides of organizer.
4. Cut three pieces of scrapbook paper to fit inside fronts of drawers; tape in place.
5. Cut scrapbook paper pieces to fit tags; tape onto tags. Print or write labels on pink cardstock; cut out and tape to tags. Tape tags to center front of each drawer.
6. Adhere IdeaStix to drawer fronts and top corners of organizer.

Corkboard Mirror,
enlarge to 160%

Whatever!
Hanging Caddy, enlarge to 126%

Beauty Secrets
Covered Boxes, enlarge to 127%

Accessory Organizer, enlarge to 123%
Clothes Hamper, enlarge to 123%
Hanging Caddy, enlarge to 155%

Three-Drawer Organizer,
enlarge to 206%

Stuff

Hanging Caddy,
enlarge to 159%

Covered Boxes

Shoe Cabinet,
enlarge to 219%

Kendra's Reading Nook

Hey, everyone.
My name is Kendra, and I lead because I read. I also love listening to music and writing poetry when the mood hits. When I'm all by myself, I want a sanctuary — a quiet spot to sort my thoughts and do my thing. BEHOLD: my reading nook!

It's all about this really huge ottoman with funky pillows and fabric-lined baskets to stow my books, tunes, and other stuff. There's even a purse CD holder revved up with paint and eyelash trim! All beneath a cozy canopy that's lit with a giant paper lantern. See it to believe it!

It's my favorite retreat of all. And just think, you can create your own cool space in a cool place, too!

Kendra

Fabric Tent

6$\frac{1}{4}$ yds dark blue
  fabric
1$\frac{1}{3}$ yds teal fabric
10 yds lime fabric
transparent tape
T-pin
yardstick
fabric marker
liquid fray preventative
2$\frac{1}{2}$ yds of $\frac{1}{2}$"w blue
  ribbon
4$\frac{1}{4}$ yds of $\frac{1}{4}$" dia.
  cotton cord
5 yds of kite string
26" dia. tubular plastic
  hoop
reinforced hook
3 yds of 2$\frac{1}{2}$"w blue
  wire-edged sheer
  ribbon
14" dia. paper lantern

Yardages are based on fabric with a 40" usable width. Match right sides and use $1/2$" seam allowance for all sewing.

1. Cut a 27" square from dark blue fabric. Follow **Cutting a Fabric Circle**, page 111, and place marker at the 14" mark to draw cutting line on fabric square. Cut out circle. Cut a hole in center of circle to accommodate lantern cord. Apply fray preventative to edges of center opening. For hanger, zigzag ends of a 5" length of $1/2$"w ribbon to edges on opposite sides of center opening.

2. For scallop border, cut a 20" x 90" piece from teal fabric (this will need to be pieced). Matching long edges, fold fabric in half. Use a photocopier to enlarge pattern, page 51, as indicated on pattern; cut out. Aligning dashed line at top of pattern along folded edge of fabric, use fabric marker to draw around scalloped edge of pattern onto fabric 10 times; cut out scallop border and set aside.

3. Cut an 18" square from dark blue fabric. For welting, follow **Continuous Bias Binding**, page 111, to cut a $1^3/4$" x 150" strip from fabric square. Center cotton cord on wrong side of strip. Matching long edges, fold fabric over cord. Use zipper foot to baste next to cord; trim excess cord.

4. Pin welting along right side of one scalloped edge. Sewing as close as possible to welting, sew scalloped edges and one end of border together. Clip curves and turn border right side out; press. Press raw edges $1/2$" to wrong side; sew opening closed.

5. Overlapping ends at back, baste scallop border around fabric circle.

6. Cut four 40" x 88" tent pieces from lime fabric. Cut two 18" x $96^1/2$" border strips and two 18" x 79" hem strips from dark blue fabric. For tent, matching wrong sides, sew tent pieces together along long edges; press seam allowances to one side. Press raw edges of seam allowances $1/4$" to wrong side; topstitch along folded edges.

7. Sew hem strips together along one end; press seam allowance open. Press one long edge of strip $1/2$" to wrong side. Matching right side of strip and wrong side of tent, sew unpressed edge of strip along bottom edge of tent. Wrapping pressed edge of hem to front of tent, pin and topstitch in place over seam. Press hem.

8. For each border along tent opening, press one end of a border strip $1/2$" to wrong side. Matching right side of strip with wrong side of tent and aligning pressed end with bottom of hem, sew one long edge of strip along side edge of tent. Press remaining long edge of strip $1/2$" to wrong side. Wrap folded edge of strip to front of tent, pin and topstitch in place over seam; press border.

9. Place string $3/8$" from top raw edge of tent; being careful not to catch string in stitching, zigzag over string using a wide stitch. Overlap tent borders by 5"; pin. Pull string to gather lime tent fabric to fit fabric circle; distributing gathers evenly, pin in place over scalloped border. Sew tent to circle; remove string.

10. Fold eight 10" lengths of $1/2$"w ribbon in half. Spacing ribbons evenly, pin folds of ribbons along tent/circle seam; topstitch. Turn tent right side out. Use ribbons to tie hoop inside tent.

11. Hang hook from ceiling. Hang tent from hook. Cut two equal lengths of $2^1/2$"w ribbon. Tie each length into a bow. Pull edge of border along tent opening back and tack bow and border in place. Run lantern cord through hole in top of tent, around hook, and behind tent to outlet.

43

Ottoman
Shown on page 42

sandpaper
round wooden coffee table
  with four legs
spray primer
navy spray paint
clear acrylic spray sealer
electric knife
6"-thick foam
transparent tape
T-pin
yardstick
fabric marker
batting
60"w teal fabric
large safety pin
$1/2$" dia. cotton cord
staple gun
fabric glue
fringe trim
beaded trim

Use spray primer, paint, and sealer in a well-ventilated area. Allow primer, paint, and sealer to dry after each application.

1. Sand legs and base of table. Prime, then paint legs and base; apply sealer.
2. Use electric knife to cut a circle from foam the same size as tabletop; place on tabletop. Measure across ottoman from bottom edge of tabletop on one side to bottom edge on opposite side. Add 6" to determined measurement and cut a square this size from batting and from fabric. Dividing determined measurement in half and adding $2^{1}/_{2}$" for marker placement, follow **Cutting a Fabric Circle**, page 111, to cut a circle from batting square. Add 1" to marker placement to cut a circle from fabric square. Press edge of fabric circle $1/4$" to wrong side. Leaving a 1"-long opening, fold and sew pressed edge $3/4$" to wrong side for casing. Use safety pin to pull cord through casing.
3. Center foam over batting; place tabletop on top of foam. Staple four opposite edges of batting to bottom of tabletop. Working on opposite sides of the tabletop and stapling in place as you go, smooth batting evenly around tabletop, folding the batting to ease in place if necessary; trim excess batting. Turn table upright.
4. Place cover on ottoman. Gathering fabric evenly, pull cord tight; knot ends together.
5. Refer to photo to layer and glue trims around sides of ottoman.

mat board
³/₈ yd black fabric
³/₈ yd teal fabric
spray adhesive
fabric glue
1³/₄ yds blue eyelash trim
white, blue, dark blue, light blue, and
 lime acrylic paints
paintbrushes
transfer paper
black paint pen
7mm crystal jewel
GemTac™ Permanent Adhesive
sandpaper
2 unfinished bell-shaped wooden purse
 handles
clear acrylic sealer
hammer and awl
blue embroidery floss
6" square black CD case

Yardages are based on fabric with a 40" usable width. Use spray adhesive in a well-ventilated area. Allow paint and sealer to dry after each application.

1. Use a photocopier to enlarge purse and CD patterns, page 51, as indicated on patterns; cut out. Use purse pattern to cut two shapes from mat board. Cut two 10" squares from each fabric. Use spray adhesive to glue a black and a teal square to opposite sides of each mat board piece. Cut edges of fabric even with edges of mat board pieces.

2. Covering raw edges of fabric, glue trim along edges of mat board with fabric glue.

3. Draw around CD pattern on teal side of one mat board piece for purse front. Using several coats, paint entire circle white. Transfer design onto white circle. Refer to photo to paint design; outline and add detail lines with paint pen. Glue jewel to center of design with GemTac.

4. Sand handles; prime with white paint. Paint handles lime, then apply sealer. Using hammer and awl to punch holes in mat board pieces, sew a handle to each piece with floss.

5. Glue black side of purse pieces to CD case with fabric glue.

YGTBK
you've got to be kidding

Tunes Groovy

rectangular baskets with handles
teal fabric
blue print fabric
air-soluble fabric
marking pen
light blue beaded trim
lime and green felt
12mm silver sequins

green miracle beads
blue-green seed beads
fabric glue
white cardboard
craft glue stick
$3/8$" dia. hole punch
dark blue beaded trim
$1/4$"w blue ribbon
blue novelty yarn

Match right sides and use $1/2$" seam allowance for all sewing.

1. To determine size of basket liner bottom, measure top edge along one end and one side of basket. Add 1" to each measurement and cut a piece from teal fabric according to determined measurements.
2. Measure the height of basket; add 2". From teal fabric, cut two side strips the determined measurement by the length of liner bottom and two end strips the determined measurement by the width of liner bottom.
3. Sew side and end strips to liner bottom (**Fig. 1**). Sew sides and ends together to make corners.

Fig. 1

4. Place liner in basket. Use fabric marking pen to mark handle placement on liner sides. Clipping fabric at corners, follow **Fig. 2** to cut away liner sides to fit around handles. Remove liner from basket. Press cut-out edges $1/4$" to wrong side; topstitch.

Fig. 2

5. For skirt of liner, measure around outer edges of basket; add 1". Cut a 6"w strip from print fabric the determined size (this strip may need to be pieced). Sew ends together to form a tube. Pin one long edge of skirt along top edge of lining; sew together, leaving pressed cut-out areas unsewn. Press raw edges of skirt at cut-out areas $1/2$" to wrong side; topstitch. Press remaining long edge of skirt $1/2$" to wrong side; topstitch. Sew light blue beaded trim along bottom edge of skirt. Place liner in basket.
6. Cut $1^1/4$" dia. circles from lime felt. Stack and sew a sequin, miracle bead, and seed bead at center of each circle; glue circles to skirt with fabric glue; allow to dry.
7. For each tag, make a color photocopy of CD, "YGTBK," or books design, page 51; cut out. Using a photocopier, enlarge tag pattern, page 51, as indicated on pattern; cut out. Use pattern to cut a tag from cardboard and green felt; glue together. Glue color photocopy to felt side of tag. Glue dark blue beaded trim across bottom of tag. Punch hole in tag according to pattern. Use ribbon and yarn to attach tag to basket handle.

Small Square Pillow

1/2 yd teal fabric
1 1/4 yds beaded trim
1 1/4 yds blue eyelash trim
lime yarn
clear nylon thread
12" square pillow form

Yardage is based on fabric with a 40" usable width. Match right sides and use 1/2" seam allowance for all sewing.

1. Cut two 13" squares from teal fabric. Refer to photo to arrange and pin trims and yarn on one square for pillow front; zigzag in place with nylon thread.

2. Leaving an opening for turning and stuffing, sew pillow front and back together. For Turkish corners, sew running stitches across each corner 1/2" from point. Gather and knot thread. Turn right side out; press.

3. Insert pillow form, then sew opening closed.

Tufted Pillow

5/8 yd blue print fabric
5/8 yd teal fabric
paper-backed fusible web
1 3/4 yds of 5/8"w lime grosgrain ribbon
fabric glue
1 3/4 yds sequin trim
18" square pillow form
1/2 yd beaded trim
four 3 1/2"-long green tassels
four green sequins
four green miracle beads
four green seed beads
2 1/2" dia. self-cover button
3 1/2" square of lime fabric
upholstery needle
heavy-duty button and upholstery
   thread
3/4" dia. button for pillow back

*Yardages are based on fabric with a 40"
usable width. Match right sides and use
1/2" seam allowance for all sewing unless
otherwise noted.*

1. Cut two 19" squares from print fabric
   and one 19" square each from teal
   fabric and fusible web. Fuse web to
   wrong side of teal piece. To make
   triangles for pillow front, cut teal
   square in half from corner to corner,
   then cut one piece again from corner
   to center of long edge. Remove
   paper backing. With points meeting
   at center of square, fuse two small
   triangles to opposite sides on right
   side of one print fabric square.
   Discard remaining triangle.

2. Forming an "X" on
   pillow front, pin two ribbon
   lengths over edges of teal
   triangles. Topstitch along
   long edges of ribbon. Glue
   sequin trim along center of ribbon
   lengths; allow to dry.

3. Leaving an opening for turning and
   stuffing, sew pillow front and back
   together. For Turkish corners, sew
   running stitches across each corner
   1/2" from point. Gather and knot
   thread. Turn right side out; press.
   Insert pillow form, then sew opening
   closed.

4. Layer and glue a length of beaded
   trim, ribbon, and sequin trim around
   top of each tassel. Twist tassel hanger
   into a tight loop. Sewing across loop,
   sew a tassel to each corner of pillow.
   Stack and sew a sequin, miracle
   bead, and seed bead over each tassel
   hanger.

5. Cover button with lime fabric; glue a
   length of beaded trim around edge
   of button back. Using heavy-duty
   thread, leaving a 5" tail, and working
   from back of pillow, insert needle
   through back button, then through
   pillow and twice around shank of
   covered button. Insert needle
   back through pillow and back
   button. Pull, then knot thread
   ends to tuft pillow; trim ends.

YGTBK Pillow
Shown on page 48

1/2 yd lime fabric
1/4 yd teal fabric
paper-backed fusible web
clear nylon thread
tissue paper
black embroidery floss
1/2 yd beaded trim
1/2 yd blue eyelash trim
translucent sequins
green miracle beads
green seed beads
12" x 16" pillow form

Yardages are based on fabric with a 40" usable width. Match right sides and use 1/2" seam allowance for all sewing unless otherwise noted.

1. Cut two 13" x 17" pieces from lime fabric and one 5" x 17" piece each from teal fabric and fusible web. Fuse web to wrong side of teal piece. Matching one long edge, fuse teal piece to right side of one lime piece for pillow front. Zigzag along top edge of teal piece with nylon thread.

2. Use a photocopier to enlarge "YGTBK" pattern, page 51, as indicated on pattern. Turn pattern over and trace "YGTBK" onto paper side of fusible web. Fuse web to wrong side of teal fabric; cut out letters and remove paper backing. Arrange and fuse letters on lime section of pillow front 2" from zigzaged teal edge.

3. Trace words onto tissue paper. Pin tissue pattern to pillow front below "YGTBK." Using three strands of floss, follow **Embroidery**, page 112, to work stem stitches over words and around "YGTBK" letters. Add French knots for dots and straight stitch for apostrophe. Gently tear away tissue paper.

4. Layer and pin trims on pillow front along top edge of teal fabric; zigzag in place with nylon thread.

5. Leaving an opening for turning and stuffing, sew pillow front and back together. For Turkish corners, sew running stitches across each corner 1/2" from point. Gather and knot thread. Turn right side out; press.

6. Refer to photo to sew sequins and beads to pillow front. Insert pillow form, then sew opening closed.

Basket Liners with Tags

CD Purse, enlarge to 248%

Fabric Tent, enlarge to 269%

YGTBK
you've got to be kidding

YGTBK Pillow,
enlarge to 400%

CD Purse, enlarge to 126%

Basket Liners with Tags,
enlarge to 200%

Chloë's Bath

I'm Chloë ... so glad you could stop by! My friends say I'm clueless and I have a heart of gold.

Anyway, let me show off a few of the cool new looks in my bathroom. It's packed with girly style and attitude. Check out my wild "doll face" makeup organizer and the perfectly pampering decorative pegs holding all my favorite bangles ... just what a fashion guru like me needs to keep myself looking my best. Right?

I glammed up a wooden tray with tiles and stickers. Now it's a regular "spa girl" special! And my shower curtain is covered with sweet red lips — a kiss of genius!

OooooK ... Just thought I'd clue you in to a few ideas for your bathroom! It's been fun. Ciao!

Chloë

4³/₄ yds orange print fabric

1 yd pink print fabric

¹/₈ yd white fabric

2¹/₂ yds of 1¹/₂"w plaid ribbon

2¹/₂ yds pink fluffy trim

paper-backed fusible web

black thread

Yardages are based on fabric with a 40" usable width. Match right sides and use a ¹/₂" seam allowance. Our two-panel shower curtain fits a 60" long rod. You may need to adjust measurements to fit your curtain rod.

1. For each panel, cut a 40" x 83" piece from orange fabric. For each casing, cut a 7" x 40" strip from pink fabric.

2. For bottom hem, press one end of panel ¹/₂" to wrong side, then press 4" to wrong side again; hem. Press sides of panel ¹/₄" to wrong side twice; topstitch. Press ends of casing ¹/₄" to wrong side twice; topstitch.

3. Sew casing along top of panel. Press remaining edge of casing ¹/₂" to wrong side, then press 3¹/₄" to wrong side again; pin in place with pressed edge of casing extending ³/₈" below seam.

4. Cut a 40" length of ribbon and a 39" length of trim for each panel. Folding ribbon ends ¹/₂" to wrong side and matching top edge of ribbon with seam between casing and panel, pin trim, then ribbon to panel. Sew along edges of ribbon, catching trim and pinned edge of casing in stitching. Topstitch 1" from top edge of casing for rod pocket.

5. Using a photocopier, enlarge pattern, page 61, as indicated on pattern. For each panel, trace enlarged pattern three times onto paper side of fusible web; cut out. Cut mouth opening from lips. Fuse lips to wrong side of pink fabric and mouth opening to wrong side of white fabric; cut out. Remove paper backing, then fuse appliqués to panel.

6. Follow **Machine Appliqué**, page 110, to sew appliqués to panel with black thread.

primer
unfinished wooden tray
lilac, white, purple, and black acrylic
  paints
paintbrushes
matte clear acrylic sealer
white glazed tiles in assorted sizes
tile adhesive
grout
soft, clean cloth
grout sealer
So Girly!™ IdeaStix™

*Allow primer, paint, and sealer to dry
after each application.*

1. Prime inner and outer sides of
   tray; paint lilac. Paint top side
   edges white. Refer to photo to
   paint animal print on inner and
   outer sides of tray. Use end of
   paintbrush handle to add black
   dots along top edges. Outline
   edges with black paint. Apply
   acrylic sealer to sides of tray.
2. Arrange tiles on tray as desired;
   secure with tile adhesive. Allow
   adhesive to set. Mix grout
   according to manufacturer's
   instructions. Being sure to fill all
   spaces between tiles, apply grout
   to tiled surface. Let grout set for
   10 minutes, then wipe off excess
   and allow to dry overnight.
3. Polish tiles with cloth, then apply
   grout sealer to tiled area. Adhere
   IdeaStix to tiles.

¹/₄ yd each pink, orange, and green print fabrics
flip-flops

1. Cut 1" x 7" strips from each fabric.
2. Alternating fabric colors, knot strips onto flip-flop straps until full. Fluff fabric strips.

Super Star

spagirl

5" x 7" wooden rectangular
  plaque
two 5" x 7" wooden oval
  plaques
drill and drill bit
three 1⅝" sawtooth hangers
primer
green, orange, light yellow,
  pink, and purple acrylic paints
paintbrushes
decoupage medium
matte clear acrylic sealer
5mm and 7mm clear jewels
GemTac™ Permanent Adhesive
3 white ceramic drawer pulls

*Allow primer, paint, decoupage
medium, and sealer to dry after
each application.*

1. Drill a hole in each plaque
    for attaching drawer pull.
    Attach a hanger to back of
    each plaque.
2. Prime plaques. Refer to
    photo to paint plaques.
3. Make a color photocopy of
    each design, page 61; cut
    out. Decoupage designs onto
    plaques; apply sealer.
4. Glue 5mm jewels to front of
    plaques and 7mm jewels
    along sides of plaques.
5. Attach a drawer pull to each
    plaque for peg.

Decorative Pegs

sandpaper
4"h wooden egg-shaped basket
8" dia. decorative wooden plate with
   scalloped edge
large wooden spoon with $3/8$" dia.
   handle
four 2"h x $1\frac{1}{2}$" dia. wooden spools with
   center holes large enough to
   accommodate spoon handle
drill and drill bit
screwdriver
#10 x $1\frac{1}{2}$" flat-head wood screw
wood glue
primer
8mm and 10mm unfinished wooden
   beads
20-gauge gold craft wire
wire cutters
green, pink, purple, orange, yellow, and
   light yellow acrylic paints
purple glass paint
paintbrushes
black fine-point permanent pen
hot glue gun
matte clear acrylic sealer
$7/8$"w ombre ribbon
scalloped-edge scissors
scrap of lime felt
$8\frac{3}{4}$" dia. beveled mirror with hanger
   removed
silicone glue
26" length of orange jumbo rickrack
pink craft foam
5" x $4\frac{1}{2}$" asymmetric wooden star
tracing paper
transfer paper
So Girly!™ IdeaStix™ flower

*Use wood glue for all gluing unless
otherwise indicated. Allow primer, paint,
and sealer to dry after each application.*

1. Lightly sand all wooden pieces. For
   stand, drill a pilot hole through
   center of basket and plate. Aligning
   holes, drive screw through front of
   plate and into bottom of basket.
2. Making sure holes are aligned, glue
   one spool inside basket. Stack and
   glue remaining spools together.
3. Apply primer to beads. String twenty
   8mm beads onto wire. Twisting wire
   ends together to secure and
   trimming excess wire, glue beads
   around edge where second and third
   spools meet. Paint nine 8mm beads
   and nine 10mm beads orange.
   Alternating small and large beads,
   string orange beads onto a $7\frac{1}{2}$"
   length of wire; set aside.
4. Apply primer to entire stand, then
   refer to photo to paint stand with
   acrylic paints, using ends of
   paintbrush handles to make dots.
   Outline dots with pen.
5. Wrap strand of orange beads around
   top of egg. Twist wire ends together
   at back; trim excess wire. Secure
   strand at back only with a dot of hot
   glue. Apply sealer to stand.
6. Overlapping ends at back and
   trimming excess ribbon, wrap a
   length of ribbon around each spool
   center; hot glue at back. Use
   scalloped-edge scissors to cut a $1/2$"w
   felt strip long enough to wrap
   around top intersection of spools.
   Glue strip in place around
   intersection.
7. Insert spoon handle in hole in center
   of stand; secure with wood glue.
8. Use glass paint and the end of a
   large paintbrush handle to paint
   purple dots around edge of mirror.
   With bottom of mirror resting on top
   spool, glue concave part of spoon to
   back of mirror with silicone glue. Hot
   glue rickrack along back edge of
   mirror. Use scalloped-edge scissors to
   cut an $8\frac{3}{4}$" dia. circle from craft
   foam; hot glue circle to back of
   mirror, covering spoon.
9. Paint entire star light yellow. Trace
   pattern, page 61, onto tracing paper.
   Transfer pattern onto star. Refer to
   photo to paint star; outline with pen.
   Adhere IdeaStix to star. Glue star to
   mirror with silicone
   glue.

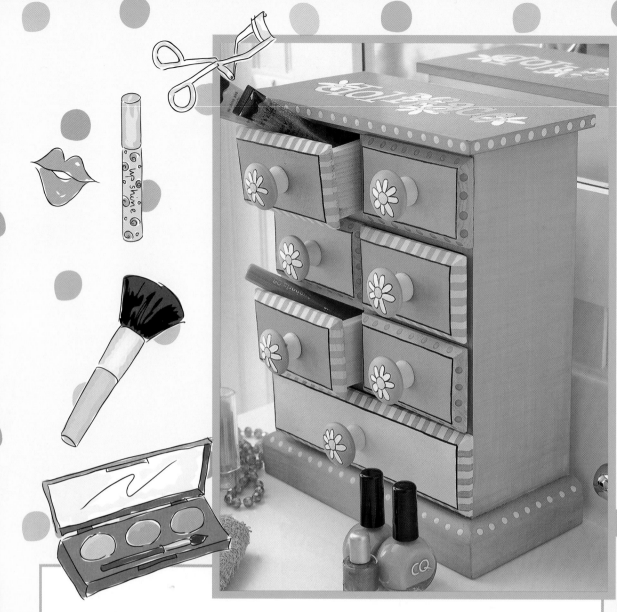

9"w x 11¹/₄"h x 4¹/₂"d unfinished
   7-drawer wooden organizer
primer
seven 1¹/₄" dia. unfinished wooden
   drawer pulls
orange, light yellow, pink, white, and
   green acrylic paints
paintbrushes
tracing paper
transfer paper
black fine-point permanent pen
matte clear acrylic sealer

*Allow primer, paint, and sealer to dry
after each application.*

1. Remove drawers from organizer;
    remove drawer pulls from drawers.
    Prime organizer, front drawer
    panels, and 1¹/₄" dia. drawer pulls.
    Refer to photo to paint organizer,
    drawers, and 1¹/₄" drawer pulls.
    Use end of paintbrush handle to
    add dots.

2. Using a photocopier, enlarge "doll
    face" pattern, page 61, as
    indicated on pattern. Transfer
    pattern onto top of organizer.
    Trace, then transfer a flower onto
    each drawer pull. Refer to photo
    to paint. Use pen to outline words,
    flowers, and front of drawer
    panels.

3. Attach painted drawer pulls to
    existing holes in drawer panels.
    Apply sealer to organizer and
    drawers; replace drawers.

Makeup Organizer

Shower Curtain, enlarge to 151%

Toll Face

Makeup Organizer,
enlarge to 110%

Princess

Mirror

Decorative
Pegs

61

Jessie's Room

I'm Jessie!
I love sports and being active. I always try to stay in shape and be on top of the trends — and it's no easy job! I wanted to invite you in for a peek at chic — my bedroom makeover. I think it's way cool!

Cargo pants are all the rage, so they're the theme of my room re-do! Check out the cargo-pocket bed skirt, my GIRL POWER wall shelf with hanging pegs, and the "Queen of the Court" tote (with a water bottle pocket!). And how about my awesome pillows and dazzling photo cubes! There's even a doggie pillow for my best pal Tucker. Everything is so worthy of a girly "Super Star!"

Jessie

white mat board
So Girly!™ green
  checked scrapbook
  paper
wooden frame with a
  6" x 7⁵/₈" opening
tracing paper
transfer paper
purple, lime, blue, light
  blue, and teal acrylic
  paints
paintbrushes
black fine-point permanent pen
primer
assorted sizes of wooden stars
hot glue gun
matte clear acrylic sealer
1 yd green eyelash trim
¹/₂ yd of ⁵/₈"w green ombre
  wire-edged ribbon

*Allow paint to dry after each
application.*

1. Cut a piece of mat board and
   scrapbook paper to fit in frame.
   Cut a 4¹/₄" x 6³/₄" opening in
   center of scrapbook paper; set
   aside.

2. Omitting star, trace pattern,
   page 79, onto tracing paper;
   transfer words onto center of mat
   board piece. Refer to photo to
   paint design; use end of
   paintbrush handle to add dots.
   Outline design with pen.

3. Prime, then refer to photo to paint
   frame and stars. Use ends of
   paintbrush handles to paint dots
   on frame. Hot glue stars to frame
   and mat board. Apply sealer to
   frame. Glue trim along edges of
   frame. For hanger, hot glue ends
   of a 15" length of ribbon to back
   of frame.

4. Insert scrapbook paper, then mat
   board in frame.

1⁷/₈ yds yellow checked fabric
transfer paper
black, white, and blue paint pens
30" square pillow form
boucle yarn

*Yardage is based on fabric with a 40"
usable width. Match right sides and use
a ¹/₂" seam allowance for all sewing.*

1. Cut two 31" squares from fabric.
2. Using a photocopier, enlarge
   patterns, page 78, as indicated on
   patterns. Transfer patterns onto one
   fabric piece for pillow front. Paint
   designs with pens; allow to dry.

3. Leaving one edge open for turning
   and inserting pillow form, sew
   pillow front and back together;
   clip corners. Insert pillow form,
   then sew opening closed.
4. Beginning and ending 2¹/₂" from
   corners on each side and leaving
   10" yarn tails, follow **Embroidery**,
   page 112, to whipstitch a length
   of yarn over each seam. Tie yarn
   tails into a bow around each
   corner; trim ends.

Cargo Pocket Pillow

⁵/₈ yd teal print fabric
¹/₄ yd blue fabric
³/₈ yd striped fabric
¹/₄ yd of beaded trim
7" and 8" blue zippers
charm with dangling stars
fabric glue
¹/₂ yd of ⁵/₈"w green ombre ribbon
³/₈ yd of 1"w lime grosgrain ribbon
³/₈ yd of 1"w navy grosgrain ribbon
iron-on monogram appliqué
2 D-rings
pinking shears
blue vinyl snap bracelet
¹/₄ yd of green eyelash trim
clear nylon thread
star button
18" square pillow form

Yardages are based on fabric with a 40" usable width. Match right sides and use a ¹/₄" seam allowance for all sewing unless otherwise noted.

1. For pillow front and back, cut two 19" squares from teal fabric.
2. For upper zipper pocket, cut a 5¹/₄" x 8¹/₂" piece from blue fabric and a 2" x 8¹/₂" piece from striped fabric. For mini pocket, cut a 3" x 3¹/₂" piece from striped fabric. Press ends and one long edge of blue piece ¹/₄" to wrong side. Repeat for 2" x 8¹/₂" striped piece. Baste an 8" length of beaded trim to raw edge on right side of blue piece. Folding ends to wrong side, sew one flange of 8" zipper over top of trim. Sew remaining flange of zipper over raw edge of striped piece. Attach charm to zipper. Press edges of mini

pocket piece ¹/₄" to wrong side; leaving top edge open, topstitch to pocket. Leaving ends of zipper unsewn, refer to **Fig. 1** to arrange and topstitch pocket to pillow front. Glue closed end of zipper to pillow front.

Fig. 1

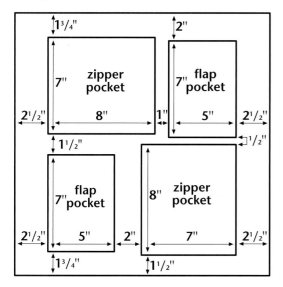

3. For lower zipper pocket, cut two 4" x 7¹/₂" pieces from blue fabric and two 2" x 7¹/₂" pieces from striped fabric. Press ends and one long edge of each blue piece ¹/₄" to wrong side. Press one long edge of each striped piece ¹/₄" to wrong side. Matching raw edges, center and pin a striped piece right side up on each blue piece; fold ends to wrong side. Topstitch along long pressed edges of striped pieces. Center a flange of 7" zipper over raw edge of each striped piece. Cut two 8" lengths of ombre ribbon. Center and pin a ribbon length over each flange of zipper. Folding ends to wrong side, topstitch along long edges of ribbon. Adhere monogram to pocket. Leaving ends of ribbon and zipper unsewn, refer to **Fig. 1** to arrange and topstitch pocket on pillow front. Glue closed end of zipper to pillow front.

4. For flap pockets, cut two 5¹/₂" x 7¹/₂" pieces and two 5¹/₂" squares from striped fabric.

5. For bottom of each flap pocket, press edges of 5¹/₂" x 7¹/₂" pieces under ¹/₄". Topstitch along one short edge of each piece. On one bottom piece, attach D-rings as follows: fold a 4" length of lime ribbon in half, forming a loop. Thread D-rings to center of loop, then fold both ribbon ends under ³/₄". Topstitch folded ends to pocket, centered 2¹/₄" from bottom edge. Refer to **Fig. 1** to arrange bottom of pockets on pillow front. Topstitch along side and bottom edges.

6. For each pocket flap, fold one 5¹/₂" square in half; sew edges at each short end together. Clip corners; turn right side out and press. Fold bottom raw edges to inside of flap; topstich. On one flap, wrapping ends of ribbon to back, cover bottom edge with a 5¹/₂" length of navy ribbon; topstitch along both edges. Use pinking shears to cut bracelet 5" long. Glue bracelet to center of ribbon. Pin one end of a 7" length of lime ribbon to wrong side of flap ¹/₄" from center top edge. Place top edge of flap ¹/₂" from edge of pocket bottom; topstitch edge in place. Thread ends of ribbon through D-rings. On other flap, zigzag eyelash trim along bottom edge with nylon thread. Sew star button to center of flap. Sew flap above remaining pocket bottom in same manner as first.

7. Leaving an opening at bottom for turning and inserting pillow form, use a ¹/₂" seam allowance to sew pillow front and back together. Clip corners and turn right side out. Insert pillow form; sew opening closed.

Star Pillow Sham
Shown on page 66

2 yds striped fabric
paper-backed fusible web
$^1/_4$ yd yellow checked fabric
black thread
fabric glue
$2^3/_4$ yds of 1"w blue grosgrain ribbon
$2^3/_4$ yds of green eyelash trim
20" x 26" pillow

Yardages are based on fabric with a 40" usable width. Match right sides and use a $^1/_2$" seam allowance for all sewing.

1. From striped fabric, cut a 25" x 31" piece for sham front and a 17" x 25" and a 21" x 25" piece for sham back.
2. Using a photocopier, enlarge star pattern, page 79, as indicated on pattern. Turn pattern over and trace onto paper side of fusible web three times. Fuse web to wrong side of checked fabric; cut out appliqués and remove paper backing. Fuse stars on sham front. Follow **Machine Appliqué**, page 110, to sew stars on sham front with black thread.
3. Press one short edge of each back piece $^1/_2$" to wrong side twice; topstitch to secure. Place back pieces on sham front with finished edges overlapping 5" at center; sew back pieces to front. Clip corners and turn sham right side out; press. Sew around sham 2" from edges, forming flange.
4. Layer and glue ribbon and trim over stitching lines along inner edges of flange. Insert pillow through back opening in sham.

Pillow with Flap
Shown on page 66

$^1/_2$ yd teal print fabric
$^1/_4$ yd yellow checked fabric
12" x 16" pillow form
fabric glue
$^1/_2$ yd of 1"w blue grosgrain ribbon
$^1/_2$ yd green eyelash trim
blue belt

Yardages are based on fabric with a 40" usable width. Match right sides and use a $^1/_2$" seam allowance for all sewing.

1. Cut two 13" x 17" pieces from teal fabric for pillow and two 5" x 17" pieces from checked fabric for flap.
2. Sew flap pieces together along ends and one long edge. Clip corners; turn right side out and press. Matching raw edges, pin flap to right side of one pillow piece for pillow front. Leaving an opening at bottom for turning and inserting pillow form and being careful not to catch ends of flap in stitching, sew pillow front and back together. Clip corners and turn right side out. Fold flap to front of pillow. Insert pillow form, then sew opening closed.
3. Folding and gluing ends to back, glue top long edge of ribbon along bottom edge of flap. Glue flange of trim to back of flap behind bottom edge of ribbon. Fasten belt around center of pillow.

magnetic paint
3 unfinished wooden boxes with lids
⅝" dia. and ¾" dia. round magnets
blue, teal, light blue, and green acrylic
  paints
paintbrushes
hot glue gun
green eyelash trim
beaded trim
boucle yarn
⅝"w green ombre wire-edged ribbon
star and flower buttons
self-adhesive magnetic sheets

Allow paint to dry after each application.

1. Prime boxes and lids with several coats of magnetic paint. Paint boxes, lids, and round magnets as desired with acrylic paints.
2. Glue trims, yarn, and ribbon to box lids as desired. Glue or sew buttons to trims.
3. For magnets, make color photocopies of the designs on page 78. Adhere photocopies to magnetic sheets and cut out. Arrange magnets on boxes.

wooden shelf with $6^3/_4$" x $19^1/_2$" insert
    and pegs
sandpaper
primer
ruler
white, green, lime, teal, light blue, and
    dark blue acrylic paints
paintbrushes
4" dia. wooden stars
transfer paper
black fine-point permanent pen
wood glue
matte clear acrylic sealer

*Allow primer, paint, and sealer to dry after
each application.*

1. Remove insert from shelf. Sand shelf
   and insert, then apply primer. Draw
   a $^3/_4$"w border on shelf around insert
   opening. Refer to photo to paint
   border, shelf, pegs, and stars. Use
   end of paintbrush handle to add
   light blue dots to border. Paint inner
   edges around insert opening green.
   Paint insert lime.

2. Using a photocopier, enlarge
   pattern, page 79, as indicated on
   pattern. Transfer pattern onto insert.
   Refer to photo to paint design. Use
   pen to outline design and painted
   border and draw circles around
   pegs. Replace insert in frame; glue
   stars to shelf.

3. Apply sealer to shelf.

1³/₄ yds cream fabric
1²/₃ yds striped fabric
³/₈ yd teal print fabric
¹/₃ yd yellow checked fabric
¹/₄ yd blue fabric
7³/₄" x 14¹/₄" piece of heavy cardboard
three 12" x 18" craft foam sheets
fabric glue
lime jumbo rickrack
fusible batting
paper-backed fusible web
compass
tracing paper
transfer paper

blue, gold, and hot pink paint pens
black fine-point permanent pen
¹/₂ yd lime mini pom-pom fringe
18" length of boucle yarn
8 silver ¹/₄" dia. grommets
   and grommet kit
³/₄ yd of ¹/₈"w blue satin ribbon
2 silver barrel beads
2 silver bell beads
¹/₂" dia. white button
1" dia. blue button
2¹/₃ yds of ⁵/₈"w sheer green checked
   ribbon

Yardages are based on fabric with a 40" usable width. Match right sides and use a 1/2" seam allowance for all sewing unless otherwise noted.

1. Cut two 24" x 36" pieces from cream fabric for lining and one 24" x 36" piece from striped fabric for bag.
2. Matching ends, fold one lining piece in half. Sew sides together. To form bottom corners, match side seams to bottom fold; sew across each corner 4" from point (**Fig. 1**). Repeat step with remaining lining piece, then bag piece. Turn bag piece right side out; do not turn linings.

Fig. 1

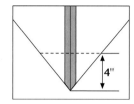

3. Place cardboard in bottom of one lining. Place second lining inside first lining. Sew linings together just past edges of cardboard. Leaving top edges open to make pockets for inserting foam, sew linings together from each bottom corner to top edge.
4. Cut two 12" x 14 1/2" pieces and two 7 1/2" x 12" pieces from foam. Insert large pieces in front and back pockets of lining and small pieces in side pockets of lining.
5. For striped pocket, cut a 14" x 19" piece from striped fabric. Matching ends, fold fabric in half; round corners opposite folded edge. Leaving an opening at bottom for turning, use a 1/4" seam allowance to sew around edges of fabric. Clip corners and curves. Turn right side out and sew opening closed; press. Glue rickrack behind folded edge.

6. Cut an 8" square each from cream fabric, batting, and fusible web. Use compass to mark a 6" dia. circle on each square; cut out. Trace pattern, page 79, onto tracing paper, then transfer pattern to center of fabric circle. Refer to photo, page 71, to paint design with paint pens; allow to dry. Outline design with permanent pen. Protecting ironing board with a scrap of fabric and sandwiching flange of pom-pom fringe between batting and web, fuse batting circle, then web circle to wrong side of fabric circle. Remove paper backing. Fuse circle onto pocket 1 1/2" from bottom and left side of pocket, then glue yarn along edge.
7. For beverage pocket, cut a 7 3/4" x 17" piece from checked fabric. Matching ends, fold fabric in half. Leaving an opening at bottom for turning and using a 1/4" seam allowance, sew around edges of fabric. Clip corners, turn right side out, and sew opening closed; press. Sew across pocket 3/4", then 1 1/4" from folded edge. Follow **Fig. 2** to attach grommets to beverage pocket between stitched lines.

Fig. 2

| 3/4" ○ | 1" | ○ | 1" | ○ | 1 3/4" | ○ | 1" | ○ | 1" | ○ 3/4" |

Attach grommets to upper right corner of striped pocket as shown in **Fig. 3**. Follow **Fig. 4** to press, then pin a 1 3/4"w pleat at center bottom of beverage pocket. Aligning end grommets on beverage pocket with grommets on striped pocket, pin beverage pocket to striped pocket; topstitch along side and bottom edges.

Fig. 3

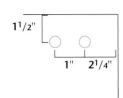

1½"
1"   2¼"

Fig. 4

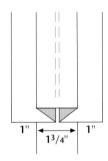

1"   1"
1¾"

8. Starting on inside of striped pocket, thread ends of a 22" length of ⅛"w ribbon through grommets. Thread barrel beads, then bell beads onto ribbon ends; knot and trim ends. Tie ribbon into a bow. For loop to stabilize beverage pocket, sew ends of a 3" length of ⅛"w ribbon to inside edge of striped pocket above center of beverage pocket. Pin striped pocket to bag front; topstitch along side and bottom edges. Catching ½" dia. button on inside of bag, sew 1" dia. button to bag front above loop on striped pocket; hook loop over 1" dia. button.

9. For band at top of bag, cut two 5" x 24" strips from teal fabric. Center and fuse a 4" x 23" strip of batting to wrong side of each strip. Sew ends of strips together to form a loop. Sew rickrack along right side of one long edge of loop.

10. Place lining in bag. Matching raw edges, pin band to outside of bag. Sew band, bag, and lining together along raw edges. Press band 2½" to inside of bag.

11. For each strap (make 2), cut a 3½" x 40" strip each from striped and blue fabric; center and fuse a 2½" x 39" strip of batting to wrong side of blue strip. Matching right sides and leaving one end open for turning, sew striped piece and blue piece together; clip corners and turn right side out. Press strap, then topstitch along edges. Zigzag both edges of a 40" length of ⅝"w ribbon along center of strap.

12. Pin 2½" of strap ends inside bag 4" from sides. Topstitch along the seam to secure band and strap ends on inside of bag. Stitch each strap to top edge of bag to secure.

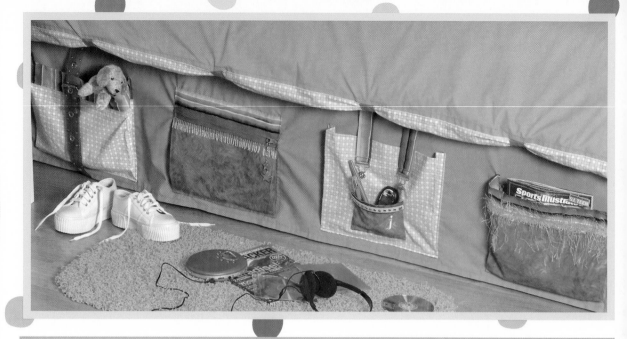

2¹/₄ yds decking
twin-size flat sheet
³/₈ yd yellow checked fabric
⁵/₈ yd striped fabric
³/₈ yd teal print fabric
¹/₂ yd beaded trim
charm with dangling stars
12" zipper
2 overall buckles with no-sew buttons
fabric glue
¹/₄ yd of 1"w navy grosgrain ribbon
pinking shears
blue vinyl snap bracelet
iron-on monogram appliqué
¹/₂ yd lime eyelash trim
⁵/₈" dia. hook-and-loop fastener
blue belt

*Yardages are based on fabric with a 40"
usable width. Match right sides and use a
¹/₂" seam allowance for all sewing unless
otherwise noted. Yardage is given to make
a three-sided bed skirt for a standard twin
bed that measures 15" from top of box
springs to floor; you may need to adjust
the amount of fabric to fit your bed.*

1. Cut a 40" x 77" piece from decking.
    For sides, cut two 16" x 77" strips
    from sheet. For end, cut a 16" x 41"
    strip from sheet. Press ends of each
    strip ¹/₂" to wrong side twice;
    topstitch to secure. For bottom hem,
    press one long edge of each strip
    ³/₄" to wrong side twice; topstitch
    to secure.

2. For belt pocket, cut a 9" x 17" piece
    from checked fabric. Cut a 5" x 17"
    strip from striped fabric for border.
    Press long edges of border strip ¹/₂"
    to wrong side. Matching wrong
    sides and pressed edges, fold strip
    in half; press. With ¹/₂" of one long
    edge of pocket piece between
    pressed edges of border, sew border
    to pocket. Press raw edges of pocket
    ¹/₂" to wrong side.

3. For zipper pocket, cut an 8¹/₂" x 17"
    piece from teal fabric. Cut a
    2¹/₂" x 13" strip from striped fabric
    for border. Press all but one long
    edge of border strip ¹/₂" to wrong
    side. Folding ends of flange to
    wrong side, sew one flange of zipper
    over long raw edge of border strip.
    Glue a length of beaded trim along
    back of remaining flange. Press all
    but one long edge of pocket piece
    ¹/₂" to wrong side. Center and sew
    beaded flange of zipper over long
    raw edge of pocket. Attach charm
    to zipper pull.

4. For overall pocket, cut an 11" x 17" piece from checked fabric. Press edges $\frac{1}{2}$" to wrong side. For straps, cut two $4\frac{1}{2}$" x 12" strips from striped fabric. Press long edges of each strap piece $1\frac{1}{2}$" to wrong side. Topstitch $\frac{1}{4}$" from each long edge of straps. Center and attach buttons 4" apart on pocket $3\frac{1}{2}$" from top edge. Thread a buckle onto center of each strap; attach buckles to buttons.

5. For mini pocket, cut a 5" x 12" piece from teal fabric. Matching ends, fold teal piece in half. Leaving an opening for turning, sew edges together. Clip corners and turn right side out; press. Sew opening closed. Folding and gluing ends to back, glue a $6\frac{1}{2}$" length of ribbon along one long edge of mini pocket for top. Use pinking shears to cut bracelet to $5\frac{3}{4}$"; glue along center of ribbon. Adhere monogram to pocket; glue mini pocket to overall pocket.

6. For pocket with eyelash trim, cut a $9\frac{1}{2}$" x 17" piece from teal fabric. For border, cut a $4\frac{1}{2}$" x 17" strip from striped fabric. Press long edges of border strip $\frac{1}{2}$" to wrong side. Matching wrong sides and pressed edges, fold border piece in half; press. With $\frac{1}{2}$" of one long edge of pocket piece between edges of border, sew border to pocket. Zigzag a 17" length of eyelash trim along bottom edge of border. Press raw edges of pocket $\frac{1}{2}$" to wrong side.

7. To pleat each pocket, follow **Fig. 1** to press a 1"w pleat in each side of pocket (for zipper pocket, do not pleat sides of border strip). Spacing pockets evenly, arrange pockets on one side piece of bed skirt $3\frac{1}{2}$" from top edge. Leaving top fold of pleats unpinned, pin pockets to side piece. Topstitch along sides of pockets. Catching pleats in stitching, topstitch along bottom edge of pockets.

Fig. 1

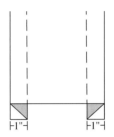

8. Beginning at fringed flange of zipper on zipper pocket, topstitch along ends and top edge of border strip. Pin ends of overall straps to top edge of side piece above overall pocket. Sew soft side of hook-and-loop fastener to center back of border on eyelash trim pocket and sew rough side to side piece of bed skirt.

9. Pin raw edges of side pieces $1\frac{1}{2}$" from one end of decking; sew in place. Pin raw edge of end piece to opposite end of decking; sew in place. Press seams to one side. Press raw edge of decking $\frac{1}{2}$", then 1" to wrong side; topstitch to secure.

10. With buckle at center, use pinking shears to cut a $14\frac{1}{2}$" length from belt. Arrange belt over pocket; glue ends to side piece and decking.

COOL

2 twin-size flat sheets
paper-backed fusible web
5/8 yd teal print fabric
7/8 yd yellow checked fabric
1/3 yd striped fabric
black thread
1/4 yd green eyelash trim
two 1 1/8" dia. star buttons
twin-size comforter
2 no-sew overall buttons

Yardages are based on fabric with a 40" usable width. Match right sides and use a 1/4" seam allowance for all sewing unless otherwise noted.

1. For duvet top and bottom, cut two 66" x 87" pieces from sheets.
2. Using a photocopier, enlarge pattern, page 79, as indicated on pattern. Turn pattern over and trace onto paper side of fusible web. Fuse words to wrong side of teal fabric and star to wrong side of checked fabric; cut out and remove paper backing. Arrange and fuse appliqués to center of duvet top. Add extra stars as desired. Follow **Machine Appliqué**, page 110, to sew appliqués with black thread.
3. For each pocket, cut a 7" x 8" piece from striped fabric. Press edges 1/4" to wrong side; topstitch along top edge. Arrange pocket on duvet top; topstitch along remaining edges.
4. For each flap, cut a 7 1/2" x 8 1/2" piece from striped fabric. Matching ends, fold flap piece in half; press. Leaving an opening for turning, sew edges together. Clip corners and turn right side out. Sew opening closed; press. Wrapping ends to back, glue a length of eyelash trim along one long edge of each flap. Sew star button to center of flap. Topstitch flap to duvet top 1/2" above pocket.
5. For teal strips on gusset (see photo, page 63), cut fourteen 3" squares from teal fabric. Press one edge of each square 3/4" to wrong side. Press opposite edge 1" to wrong side. Topstitch along center of each strip.

6. For gusset, piecing as necessary, cut a 4" x 240" strip from checked fabric. With right sides up and matching raw edges and spacing strips as shown in **Fig. 1**, baste teal strips to gusset strip. Pin, then using a 1/2" seam allowance, sew gusset strip to side and bottom edges of duvet top; clip corners and press. Pin, then sew gusset to duvet bottom; clip corners and press.

Fig. 1

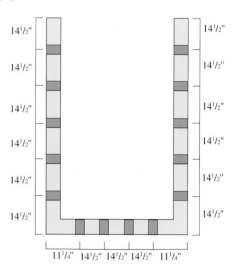

7. For ties, cut eight 3" x 8 1/4" strips from teal fabric. Matching long edges, sew side and one end of each strip together; clip corners, turn, and press. Press edges of duvet opening 3/4" to wrong side twice. Beginning and ending 10" from edge of gusset, pin raw edges of ties across from each other at 15" intervals along inside top edges of duvet. Topstitch around duvet opening 1/2" from pressed edges. Turn duvet right side out; attach overall buttons at bottom corners of duvet. Insert comforter in duvet, then knot ties together.

Woof

Magnetic Photo Cubes

tomboy

Friends

Woof

Tucker's Bed,
enlarge to 120%

Star Pillow Sham (Star only),
enlarge to 340%

Duvet Cover,
enlarge to 340%

Super Star Sign,
use at 100%

Super Star

Tote Bag

Queen of the Court

Girl Power

Girl Power Shelf, enlarge to 205%

79

Destiny's Corner

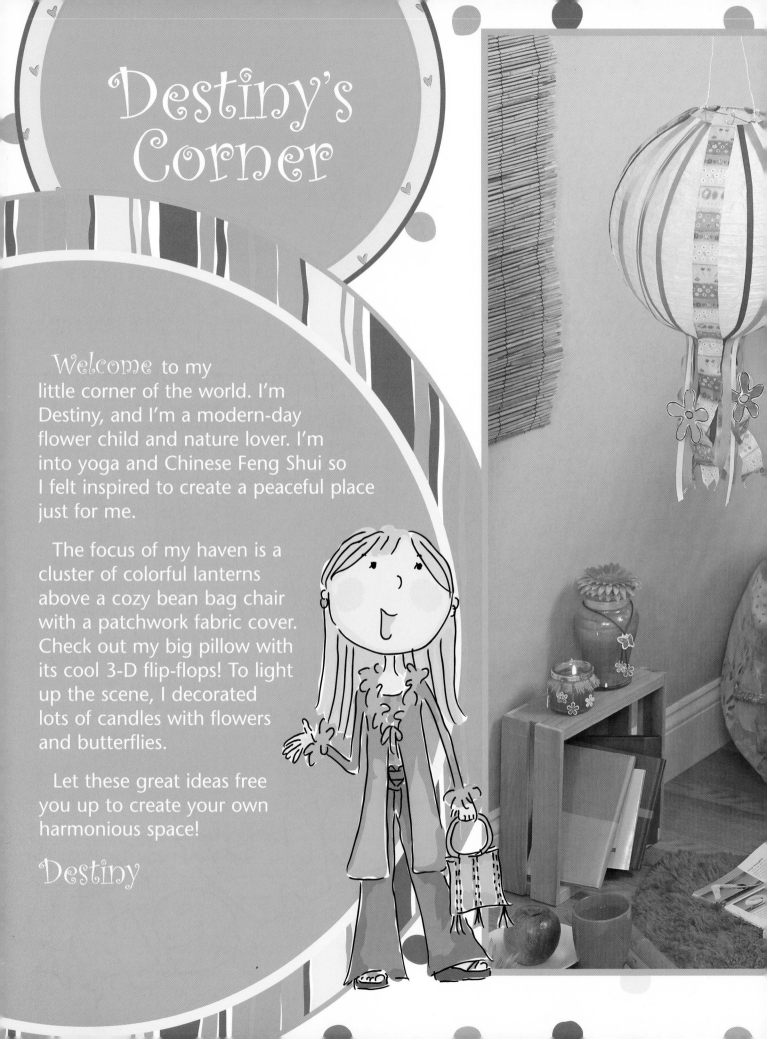

Welcome to my little corner of the world. I'm Destiny, and I'm a modern-day flower child and nature lover. I'm into yoga and Chinese Feng Shui so I felt inspired to create a peaceful place just for me.

The focus of my haven is a cluster of colorful lanterns above a cozy bean bag chair with a patchwork fabric cover. Check out my big pillow with its cool 3-D flip-flops! To light up the scene, I decorated lots of candles with flowers and butterflies.

Let these great ideas free you up to create your own harmonious space!

Destiny

28" dia. bean bag chair
tissue paper
$3^1/_3$ yds ready-made patchwork fabric
$5/_8$ yd of $3/_4$"w hook-and-loop fastener
  strip
$1/_8$ yd fabric for handles

*Yardages are based on fabric with a 40"
usable width. Our bean bag chair has
circular panels at the top and bottom and
four side panels. Adjust the amount of
fabric and shape of the pattern pieces as
needed. Match right sides and use a $1/_2$"
seam allowance for all sewing.*

Fig. 1

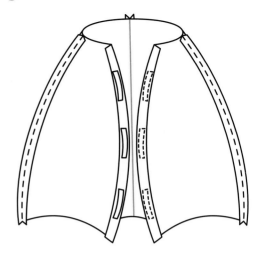

1. Using the bean bag chair as a guide,
   trace top and bottom circles and one
   side panel onto tissue paper for
   pattern pieces. Cut each circle and
   two side pieces from patchwork
   fabric $1/_2$" larger than patterns on all
   edges. Cut two remaining side pieces
   $1/_2$" larger than pattern on top and
   bottom edges and 1" larger than
   pattern on each side edge.
2. Press one long edge of one large side
   piece 1" to wrong side (**Fig. 1**).
   Repeat on opposite long edge of
   other large side piece. Leaving
   pressed edges unsewn, sew side
   pieces together; clip curves. Cut three
   7" lengths from fastener strip. Refer
   to **Fig. 1** to pin fastener strips along
   pressed edges. Catching edges of
   strips in stitching, topstitch $1/_4$" and
   $3/_4$" from each pressed edge.

3. Securing fasteners, sew top circle to
   top edge of side piece and bottom
   circle to bottom edge of side piece;
   clip curves and turn cover right side
   out.
4. For each handle, cut a $3^1/_2$" x $9^1/_2$"
   strip from handle fabric. Press ends
   $1/_2$" to wrong side. Matching long
   edges, fold strip in half. Sew long
   edges together; turn right side out.
   Matching long edges, fold handle in
   half again; pin edges $2^1/_4$" from each
   end. Topstitch long edges together
   between pins. Flatten each end of
   handle. Topstitch ends of handles
   securely on opposite sides of cover.
   Place bean bag in cover.

Flowers and Butterflies:
  craft glue
  white cardstock
  $1/16$" dia. hole punch
  spray adhesive
  clear embossing powder
  embossing heat tool
Tassels:
  sandpaper
  primer
  Create-A-Tassel wooden tassel top
  assorted acrylic paints
  paintbrushes
  matte clear acrylic sealer
  assorted yarns or embroidery floss,
    ribbon scraps, and fabric strips
  8" square of cardboard
Pink Lantern:
  pink taro paper lantern
  pink embroidery floss

hot glue gun
$7/8$ yd of $3^1/2$"-long pink eyelash trim
$1^3/4$ yds of $1^1/2$"w floral print wire-
  edged ribbon
White Lantern:
  white globe paper lantern
  $1^1/2$"w floral print wire-edged ribbon
  assorted widths of orange and hot
    pink satin ribbons
  $3/8$"w orange, yellow, and red
    grosgrain ribbons
  craft glue
Yellow Lantern:
  yellow globe paper lantern
  $1/4$"w fusible web tape
  20" square of ready-made patchwork
    fabric
  lightweight fusible interfacing
  $2^1/2$ yds of 5"-long pink eyelash trim
  fabric glue

Use spray adhesive in a well-ventilated area. Use caution when working with embossing heat tool. Allow paint and sealer to dry after each application. If desired, follow manufacturer's instructions to attach a light kit made for paper lanterns inside lantern.

1. For embossed flowers and butterflies, make a color photocopy of designs, page 89; glue photocopy to cardstock and cut out designs. Punch a hole at top of each design. Apply spray adhesive to front of each design; sprinkle embossing powder over adhesive. Shake off excess powder. Follow manufacturer's instructions to heat powder with embossing tool.

2. For each tassel, sand, then prime wooden tassel top. Refer to photo to paint top. Apply sealer. Following manufacturer's instructions, make tassel by wrapping yarns or floss, ribbon, and fabric strips around cardboard square. Slide tassel into tassel top.

3. For pink lantern, thread floss through hole in each embossed design; knot end. Trim floss to desired length and hot glue remaining end to lantern. Measure around top rim of lantern; add 3". Cut a length each of eyelash trim and wire-edged ribbon the determined length; twist ribbon. Hot glue trim, then twisted ribbon along rim. Hot glue additional ribbon around lantern as desired. Attach tassel to wire at bottom of lantern.

4. For white lantern, measure globe from top to bottom; add 10". Cut ribbons the determined length. Fold and glue one end of each ribbon to inside top rim of lantern; glue ribbon to bottom rim of lantern. Thread each embossed design onto a ribbon; knot ribbon. Trim ribbon ends.

5. For yellow lantern, fuse web tape along two opposite edges on wrong side of fabric square. Remove paper backing and press edges $1/2$" to wrong side. Repeat for remaining edges. Cut a 9" square from interfacing. Cut a $6^1/2$" dia. circle each from center of fabric and interfacing squares. Matching right sides and edges of circles, pin interfacing to fabric square. Using a $1/4$" seam allowance, sew pieces together along circles. Clip curves and trim interfacing 1" from seam. Turn interfacing to wrong side of fabric square; fuse. Glue eyelash trim around edges of fabric square. Place square over top of globe. Attach tassel to wire at bottom of lantern.

fine-grit sandpaper
canvas white Poly Shrink™ plastic sheets
transfer paper
black fine-point permanent pen
pink, cream, and orange acrylic paints
paintbrushes
$3/8$" dia. hole punch
embossing heat tool
$2^1/_2$" dia. wooden ball
three 4" dia. jar candles with lids
two $2^1/_2$" dia. jar candles
orange and pink seed beads
assorted orange and pink beads
26-gauge silver wire
hot glue gun
pink fringe
pink thread
$3/8$"w print ribbon
red satin cord
orange silk gerbera daisy
$4^1/_8$ yds each of 2"w sheer pink and
    orange ribbon
pink pony beads

Never leave burning candles unattended.
Allow paint to dry after each application.
Use caution when working with embossing
heat tool.

1. To make charms, sand plastic sheet
   with a crisscross motion. Using a
   photocopier, copy patterns, page 89,
   as indicated on patterns. Transfer
   patterns onto plastic the desired
   number of times. Draw over lines
   with pen. Using a thin wash of paint,
   refer to photo to paint charms. Cut
   out designs and punch holes as
   desired.

2. Follow manufacturer's instructions to
   heat painted charms with embossing
   tool until they shrink to half their
   original size. Handling hot charms
   carefully, shape charms over ball
   while still pliable to give them a
   slightly rounded shape.

3. For each beaded candle, string beads
   on wire and twist wire into a ring
   around jar; twist wire ends together
   to secure. Hot glue charms to jar.

4. For candle with fringe, cut fringe to
   fit around lip of jar. To add each
   charm, sew one end of thread to
   flange of fringe. Thread seed beads,
   then charm onto thread; run needle
   back through beads and knot to
   secure. Hot glue fringe, then $3/8$"w
   ribbon around lip of jar.

5. For candle with daisy, thread both
   ends of a length of satin cord
   through butterfly charm. Thread
   each end of cord through a daisy
   charm; knot ends. Place cord around
   jar. Hot glue daisy to jar lid.

6. For candle with ribbon ring, cut a
   25" length of satin cord. Cut twelve
   12" lengths each from pink and
   orange ribbon. Thread a pony bead
   on cord. Matching ends, fold an
   orange ribbon length in half. Use a
   lark's head knot to tie ribbon on cord
   (**Fig. 1**). Alternating ribbon colors,
   continue threading beads and tying
   ribbons on cord. Wrap cord around
   jar; tie ends into a bow at back. Trim
   ribbon ends and sew charms to
   ribbons as desired.

Fig. 1

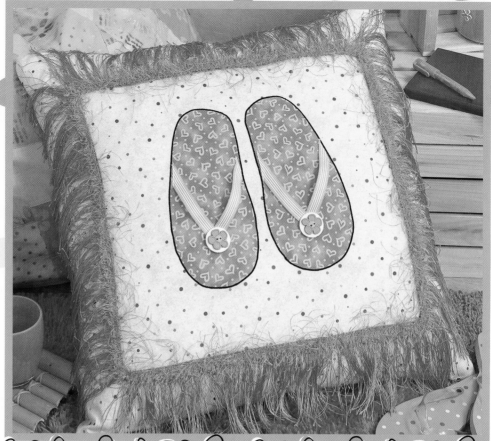

paper-backed fusible web
¹/₄ yd pink print fabric
two 25" squares of dotted yellow fabric
   for pillow front and back
black thread for appliqués
four 5" lengths of ⁵/₈"w pink ribbon
two 1¹/₈" dia. flower buttons
two 1¹/₄" dia. white buttons
24" square pillow form
2 yds of 5"-long pink eyelash trim
2 yds of 3¹/₂"-long pink eyelash trim
fabric glue

*Yardages are based on fabric with a 40"
usable width. Match right sides and use a
¹/₂" seam allowance for all sewing.*

1. Fuse web to wrong side of pink print
   fabric. Using a photocopier, enlarge
   pattern, page 89, as indicated on
   pattern. Use pattern to cut two flip-
   flops (one in reverse) from fabric. Cut
   out appliqués along drawn lines;
   remove paper backing. Arrange and
   fuse appliqués on pillow front.

2. Follow **Machine Appliqué**,
   page 110, to sew flip-flops on pillow
   front. Arrange ribbon lengths on flip-
   flops; trim ends. Sew ribbon ends
   and buttons to pillow front.

3. Leaving an opening for turning and
   stuffing, sew pillow front and back
   together. Clip corners and turn right
   side out; press. Insert pillow form,
   then sew opening closed.

4. Layer and glue trims around pillow
   front 4" from seams.

Flip-Flop Pillow, enlarge to 250%

Decorated
Lanterns

Jar Candles, enlarge butterfly to 183%,
use flower at 100% and enlarge to 167%

Jade's Phone Booth

Hi. I'm Jade ...
and this is my portable pet, Mo-Fish. I love people, edgy fashions, funky glasses, and — best of all — my Palm Pilot.

The word is out: a girl's gotta have a cool phone ... and an awesome place to call home. Voilà! Check out my phone booth, complete with a gossip bench. It has a comfy cushion for my long conversations ... and the fabric-paneled room divider gives me some privacy! My slam journal is always ready for another entry, and my memo board, with fun pushpins, is a great place to keep phone numbers, pictures, and calendar events.

Is this cool or what! Oh, gotta go — Hello ...

Jade

sandpaper
primer
wooden "step" table
lime, white, hot pink, orange, and
 yellow acrylic paints
paintbrushes
transfer paper
black fine-point permanent pen
matte clear acrylic sealer
3"-thick foam for cushion
daisy print fabric
$1/4$" dia. cotton cord
green print fabric
ten $7/8$" dia. yellow buttons
heavy-duty button and upholstery
 thread
upholstery needle

*Match right sides and use a $1/2$" seam
allowance for all sewing. Allow primer,
paint, and sealer to dry after each
application.*

1. Sand, then prime table. Paint
   tabletop lime and rest of table white.
2. Using a photocopier, reduce pattern,
   page 99, as indicated on pattern.
   Transfer pattern onto tabletop. Refer
   to photo to paint design; outline
   design with pen. Apply sealer to
   table.
3. For cushion, measure "step" of table
   from front to back and side to side.
   Cut a piece of foam the determined
   measurements. For top and bottom
   of cover, cut two pieces of daisy
   fabric 1" larger than determined
   measurements.

4. For side of cover, measure around
   sides of foam piece; add 1". Cut a
   4"w strip from daisy fabric the
   determined measurement. Sew ends
   together to form a loop.
5. For each welting length, measure
   around edges of one cover piece;
   add 3" and cut a piece of cord that
   length. Cut a $2^1/2$"w bias strip from
   green fabric the length of the cut
   cord (this strip may be pieced if
   necessary). Press one end of bias strip
   $1/2$" to wrong side. Beginning $1/2$"
   from pressed end, center cord on
   wrong side of bias strip. Matching
   long edges, fold strip over cord.
   Using zipper foot, sew next to cord.
   Trim flange of welting to $1/2$".
6. Beginning and ending 2" from
   welting ends and matching raw
   edges, pin flange of one welting
   length to right side of cover top.
   Trimming to fit, insert unfinished end
   of welting into folded end. Finish
   pinning welting to fabric; baste. Clip
   seam allowances at corners. Repeat
   with remaining welting length on
   cover bottom.
7. Sew side loop to all edges of cover
   top; clip corners.
8. Leaving one edge open for inserting
   cushion, sew side loop to cover
   bottom. Clip corners and turn right
   side out. Insert foam, then sew
   opening closed.
9. For each button set, using heavy-
   duty thread and leaving a 5" tail,
   insert needle through a button on
   bottom of cushion, then through
   cushion and through a button on
   top of cushion. Insert needle back
   through top button, cushion, and
   bottom button. Pull, then knot
   thread ends to tuft cushion.

Hello!

yakity yak

best friends

MEXICO

24" x 36" framed corkboard with
  1"w frame
white primer
hot pink, white, orange, light blue,
  lime, and dark green acrylic paints
paintbrush
matte clear acrylic sealer
painter's masking tape
spray adhesive
22" x 34" piece of batting
Perfect Glue™
22" x 34" piece of green print fabric
3 yds of $1^1/_2$"w wire-edged pink
  striped ribbon
$3^3/_8$ yds of $^7/_8$"w daisy ribbon
$^3/_4$"w fusible web tape
tracing paper
transfer paper
yellow craft foam
black fine-point permanent pen
dimensional foam dots
So Girly!™ stickers
craft plastic
pushpins

*Allow primer, paint, and sealer to dry
after each application. Use spray
adhesive in a well-ventilated area.*

1. Prime, then paint frame hot
    pink. Apply sealer to frame.
2. Cover frame with masking tape.
    Spray cork section with adhesive;
    adhere batting to board. Apply
    Perfect Glue around edges of
    batting; glue fabric to batting.

3. Cut four 9" and four 17" lengths
    of pink ribbon. Leaving a 7"
    section at center of ribbon, make
    two knots in each long length;
    knot short lengths at center.
    Glue ends of a long and short
    ribbon length across each corner
    of board. Cut two $23^1/_2$" and
    two $35^1/_2$" lengths of daisy
    ribbon; press ends under $^1/_2$".
    Slightly covering inner edges of
    frame, fuse daisy ribbon along
    edges of corkboard.
4. Trace pattern, page 99, onto
    tracing paper. Transfer pattern
    onto craft foam. Refer to photo
    to paint design. Outline design
    with pen; cut out. Adhere design
    to board with foam dots.
5. Adhere stickers to craft plastic;
    cut out. Use Perfect Glue to
    adhere plastic pieces to tops of
    pushpins.

Room Divider

wooden-framed three-panel room
   divider with spring rods
$3/4$ yd yellow print fabric
$1/2$ yd purple fabric
$1/2$ yd hot pink fabric
$1/2$ yd orange fabric
$1^1/2$ yds daisy print fabric
$1/2$ yd green print fabric
tracing paper
transfer paper
hot pink, orange, lime, purple, and
   yellow acrylic paints
paintbrushes
black paint pen
$1/2$"w fusible web tape
$1/3$ yd purple beaded trim
$1/3$ yd of $1^1/2$"w pink striped ribbon
$2^3/4$ yds of $7/8$"w daisy ribbon
fabric glue
$2^3/4$ yds yellow fuzzy trim

*Yardages are based on fabric with a 40"
usable width. The finished size for each
of our panels is 15" x 66". Adjust fabric
sizes as needed to fit your room divider.
Match right sides and use a $1/4$" seam
allowance for all sewing. Allow paint to
dry after each application.*

1. Remove panels from divider. Cut
   one 16" x 24$3/4$" piece each from
   yellow, purple, hot pink, and
   orange fabrics and two from daisy
   print fabric. Cut one 16" x 22$1/2$"
   piece from green print fabric and
   two from daisy print fabric.
2. Trace flower pattern, page 99,
   onto tracing paper. Transfer
   pattern onto yellow and orange
   fabric pieces. Refer to photo to
   paint designs; outline designs with
   paint pen.
3. For pocket, cut a 10" x 20" piece
   from yellow fabric. Matching ends
   and wrong sides, fold piece in half.
   Layer and fuse a 10" length each
   of beaded trim and striped ribbon
   along folded end. Press raw edges
   of pocket $1/2$" to wrong side.

4. Trace word pattern, page 99, onto
   tracing paper. Transfer pattern
   onto center of pocket; draw over
   transferred lines with paint pen.
   Center pocket on green piece;
   topstitch along side and bottom
   edges.
5. Refer to photo and **Fig. 1** to sew
   panel pieces together; press seams
   to one side. Fuse long edges of
   each panel $1/2$" to wrong side.
   Press top and bottom ends of each
   panel $1/2$", then 2" to wrong side.
   Topstitch 1$3/4$" from pressed ends
   for rod casings.

Fig. 1

16" x 24$3/4$"
16" x 22$1/2$"
16" x 24$3/4$"

6. Fusing ribbon ends to back of
   panel, fuse a 16" length of daisy
   ribbon over each seam between
   fabric pieces. Glue a 15" length of
   fuzzy trim over stitching on each
   rod casing. Secure panels in room
   divider.

6¼" x 7½" notebook with double-loop
   wire binding
orange acrylic paint
paintbrushes
matte clear acrylic sealer
double-stick tape
⅓ yd purple beaded trim
⅓ yd of 1½"w hot pink wire-edged
   ribbon
⅓ yd of ⅞"w daisy ribbon
tracing paper
transfer paper
black paint pen
So Girly!™ stickers
purple cardstock
So Girly!™ decorative tape

Allow paint and sealer to dry after each application.

1. Remove cover from notebook; paint cover orange. Apply sealer to cover. Replace cover on notebook.
2. Wrapping ends to inside, layer and use double-stick tape to adhere a 9½" length each of beaded trim, pink ribbon, and daisy ribbon to cover along edge of binding (if necessary, remove beads from trim on inside of cover).
3. Trace pattern, page 99, onto tracing paper. Transfer pattern onto cover; draw over transferred lines with pen. Adhere stickers to cover.
4. Use double-stick tape to adhere a 5¼" x 7¼" piece of cardstock to inside of cover. Adhere a length of decorative tape along outer edge of each notebook page.

Gossip Bench,
reduce to 75%
Room Divider,
use at 100%

Memo Board

Brooke's Study

Hi. Welcome to my Study. I'm Brooke, and I love the great outdoors — it's my nature. I climb big rocks and collect little ones!

When it's time for serious studying, I hang out in my retreat. My study desk has a unique So Girly!™ style and the matching director's chair helps me stay focused on what I'm supposed to be doing, "Studying!" Check out the three decorated containers for pens, markers, and scissors to keep me organized, and don't tell anyone, but I've got a cool hidden compartment in my desk lamp.

Whoops! Study break is over ... see ya later.

Brooke

director's chair with removable natural
   cotton canvas seat and back
transfer paper
light blue, lime, green, purple, and
   black acrylic paints
paintbrushes
assorted sizes of round foam brushes
$^5/_8$ yd striped fabric
fabric glue
$1^5/_8$ yds of $^3/_8$"w purple ribbon

Yardage is based on fabric with a 40"
usable width. Allow paint to dry after
each application.

1. Remove canvas seat and back from
   chair. Using a photocopier, enlarge
   "Study!" pattern, page 109, as
   indicated on pattern. Transfer
   pattern onto back of canvas back.
   Refer to photo to paint, then outline
   design. Use foam brushes to paint
   dots on chair back.

2. Cut a piece from striped fabric 2"
   larger than width and height of
   canvas seat. Press long edges $^1/_2$" to
   wrong side. Center canvas seat on
   wrong side of fabric; wrap and glue
   fabric edges to back.

3. Replace seat and back on chair. Cut
   ribbon length in half; tie into a bow
   around each side of chair back
   frame.

primer
unfinished wooden desk
lime, purple, light blue, and green
  acrylic paints
paintbrushes
craft glue
matte clear acrylic sealer
lime eyelash trim

Allow primer, paint, and sealer to dry after each application.

1. Prime desk, then refer to photo to paint desk. Use ends of paintbrush handles to paint dots.
2. Resizing as needed to fit your desk, use a color photocopier to copy desired designs from pages 108-109; cut out. Arrange and glue designs on desk. Apply sealer to desk.
3. Glue trim around legs of desk as desired.

Supply Organizers

So Girly!™ scrapbook paper
purple cardstock
So Girly!™ alphabet stickers
spray adhesive
clear acrylic pails
lilac beaded fringe
lime eyelash trim
craft glue

Use spray adhesive in a well-ventilated area.

1. For each label, cut a 1¹/₂" x 5" strip from scrapbook paper and a 1" x 3¹/₂" strip from cardstock. Add stickers to cardstock; trim as needed. Using spray adhesive, center and glue cardstock strip on paper strip.

2. Use spray adhesive to adhere labels to pails.

3. Cut two lengths of beaded fringe and one length of eyelash trim to fit around rim of each pail. Sandwiching eyelash trim between beaded fringe lengths, use craft glue to glue fringe and trim around rim of pail; allow to dry.

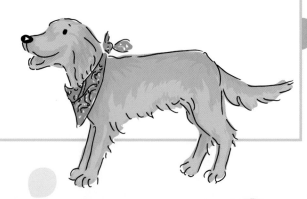

five ³/₈"-thick by 3³/₄" dia. papier-mâché ornaments
blue, lime, and purple acrylic paints
paintbrushes
matte clear acrylic sealer
poster board
lime metal spray paint
clock kit
tracing paper
transfer paper
black fine-point permanent pen
craft glue
lime yarn
8 small rhinestones
3" dia. circle punch
self-stick dry-erase roll
¹/₄" dia. hole punch

Use spray paint in a well-ventilated area. Allow paint and sealer to dry after each application.

1. Remove hangers from ornaments. For petals, paint the ornaments purple; apply sealer.

2. For clock face, cut a 4¹/₂" dia. circle from poster board. Paint circle lime. Spray paint clock hands. Trace flower pattern, page 109, four times, then refer to photo and transfer patterns onto clock face. Paint flowers; outline with pen. Apply sealer to clock face. Glue yarn around edges of clock face and rhinestones at the hours.

3. Punch five 3" dia. circles from dry-erase roll; adhere a circle to each petal.

4. Punch a hole through center of clock face. Following manufacturer's instructions, attach clock to clock face.

5. Using a photocopier, enlarge base pattern, page 109, as indicated on pattern. Transfer pattern onto poster board; cut out. Arrange and glue petals on base and clock face on petals.

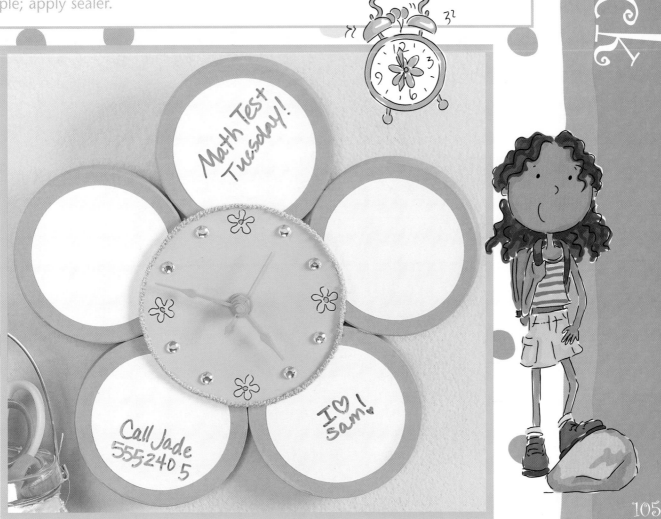

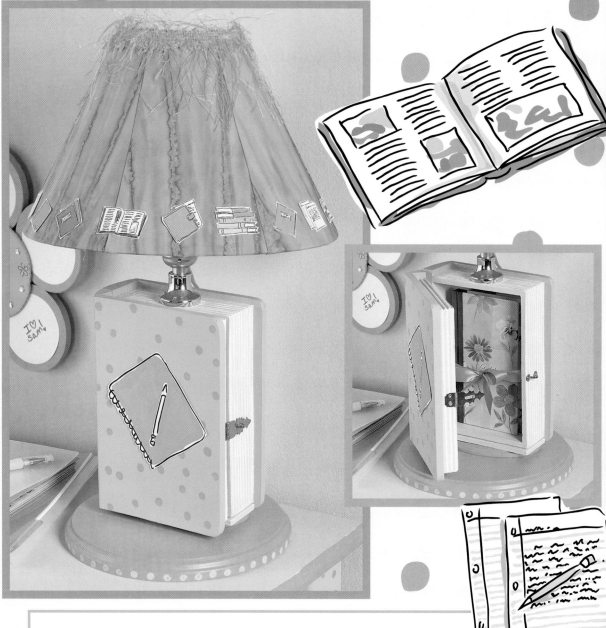

6" x 8" x 3" hinged wooden book
  box
wooden ruler
craft saw
hot glue gun
sandpaper
primer
8¹/₂" dia. wooden plaque
3¹/₂" x 5" oval wooden plaque
light blue, lime, green, yellow, white,
  and purple acrylic paints
paintbrushes
¹/₄" dia. round foam brush
matte clear acrylic sealer

#9 x 1" wood screws
  and screw driver
decorative brass hasp with staple
¹/₂ yd of ⁵/₈"w green ribbon
2 thumbtacks
craft glue
drill with ¹/₄" bit
bottle adapter lamp kit
4" dia. x 7³/₄"h x 11" dia. self-
  adhesive lamp shade
¹/₂ yd green striped fabric
¹/₄"w fusible web tape
¹/₂ yd lime eyelash trim

Yardage is based on fabric with a 40" usable width. Allow primer, paint, and sealer to dry after each application. Use craft glue unless otherwise indicated.

1. To make bottom of book box level, butt ruler against bottom of spine and back cover of book. Mark ruler at end of pages; use saw to cut along drawn line. Hot glue ruler to bottom of book box.

2. Sand, then prime wooden pieces. Paint plaques purple; use foam brush to paint light blue dots around edge of round plaque. Paint book jacket lime with green dots on covers. Paint pages and inside of book yellow with white highlights along edges of pages. Apply sealer to wooden pieces.

3. Hot glue oval plaque to round plaque (**Fig. 1**). Making sure that front of book does not hit edge of plaque when closed, hot glue ruler at bottom of book to oval plaque. Drive screws through plaques into bottom of book.

Fig. 1

$1^1/_2$"

$3^1/_2$"

4. Refer to photo to attach hasp and staple to side of pages. Cut ribbon length in half. Use thumbtacks to attach one end of each ribbon length to inner sides of back pages. Tie remaining ends into a bow.

5. Use color photocopier to copy designs, pages 108-109, as indicated on design pages; cut out designs. Glue notebook design to center front of book box.

6. Drill hole through center top of back pages. Insert threaded pipe from lamp kit in hole; hot glue to secure. Discarding rubber components, follow manufacturer's instructions to assemble lamp.

7. Remove paper covering from shade; fold into six equal sections. Add 1" to width and 2" to height of one section; cut six fabric pieces the determined size. Press left edge of each piece $^3/_8$" to wrong side for seam allowance; center fusible tape on seam allowance. Remove paper backing from one piece and fuse along right vertical edge of second fabric piece. Repeat with remaining pieces, adjusting last overlap to fit snuggly on shade.

8. Hot glue top and bottom edges of fabric to inside of shade. Cut a 1" x 16" bias strip of fabric; matching long edges, fold in half and hot glue over top rim of shade. Hot glue trim around top rim of shade. Glue design cutouts above lower rim of shade.

Desk

study

Chair, enlarge to 204%

Clock, enlarge to 218%

Clock, use at 100%

Desk, use at 100%

Desk Lamp, enlarge to 122%

Desk Lamp, use at 100%

General Instructions

Machine Appliqué

1. Place a stabilizer, such as paper, on wrong side of background fabric. Set sewing machine for a medium-width zigzag stitch (approximately $1/8$") and a very short stitch length. Set upper tension slightly looser than for regular stitching.

2. Beginning on as straight an edge as possible, position fabric so that most of the satin stitching will be on the appliqué piece. Do not backstitch; hold upper thread toward you and sew over it two or three stitches to anchor thread. Following Steps 3-6 for stitching corners and curves, stitch over exposed raw edges of appliqué pieces.

3. (Dots on Figs. indicate where to leave needle in fabric when pivoting.) For **outside corners**, stitch just past the corner, stopping with the needle in **background** fabric (**Fig. 1**). Raise presser foot. Pivot project, lower presser foot, and stitch adjacent side (**Fig. 2**).

4. For **inside corners**, stitch just past the corner, stopping with the needle in the **appliqué** fabric (**Fig. 3**). Raise presser foot. Pivot project, lower presser foot, and stitch adjacent side (**Fig. 4**).

Fig. 3   Fig. 4

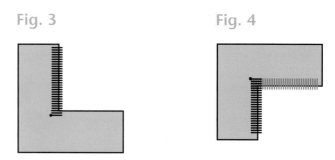

5. When stitching **outside curves**, stop with needle in **background** fabric. Raise presser foot and pivot project as needed. Lower presser foot and continue stitching, pivoting as often as necessary to follow curve (**Fig. 5**).

Fig. 5

Fig. 1   Fig. 2

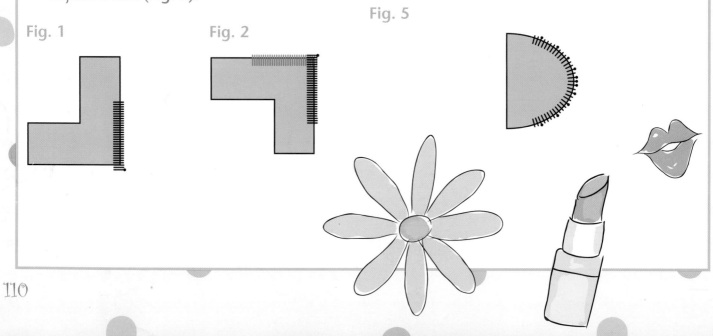